GOLDEN YEARS

SAM C. RAMEY

GOLDEN YEARS

SAM C. RAMEY

ABOOKS
Alive Book Publishing

Golden Years

Additional copies may be ordered from the publisher for educational, business, promotional or premium use. For information, contact ALIVE Book Publishing at:
alivebookpublishing.com

ISBN 13
978-1-63132-273-0

First Edition

Published in the United States of America by ALIVE Book Publishing
an imprint of Advanced Publishing LLC
3200 A Danville Blvd., Suite 204, Alamo, California 94507
alivebookpublishing.com

PRINTED IN THE UNITED STATES OF AMERICA

10 9 8 7 6 5 4 3 2 1

The inspiration to write this book was given to me by my mother. She was Stella Peteet Ramey. Some of these happenings were told to her at an early age but she lived during the time when a lot of the events were taking place.

This was an important time in the life of the South and it was also a valuable time in my mother's life. She was happy to be a part of that era, but she wanted people to be able to read about it. She was never able to put the happenings together so that is why it was important for me to write this story.

To those who knew her closely, she wanted them to call her "Mammy," as she knew and was cared for by a negro mammy and she had a great love for them.

To not have written this book would have left out a part of the South in time of slavery and the pioneers who were before them.

In relating these happenings and events, it gives a better prospective on slavery and the South. How it grew ad prospered in the good times and suffered in the bad times.

PREFIX

The first slaves to cross the Atlantic Ocean arrived in Spain in 1492.

They were American Indians. They were brought over by Columbus.

Columbus came looking for gold but did not find it or much else, except Indians. So to compensate for the expenses that Queen Isabelle and King Ferdinano had furnished for the ships, he returned with Indian slaves.

The next slaves were the Indenturies. They were mostly European whites. They did not have passage to the new world so they had to work this debt off to the land owner. This took about seven years which was required to pay this debt.

The next slaves were the negros from Africa. In 1619 there were approximately thirty slaves that arrived in Virginia by a Dutch ship.

Tobacco was the main crop at this time.

A short time later cotton became king. It had to be produced in large quantity and by cheap labor.

Seeds could not be removed from the cotton successfully, but in 1793 E. Whitney invented the cotton gin.

Factories in England purchased as much cotton as was available. It was also in demand in the mills in the northern states.

This propelled the South's prosperity in the world unknown. It was referred to as the "Golden Years."

For the plantation owner it was wealth and more wealth.

The North and South could not resolve their differences and this brought on the war.

The war caused the South to plunge into severe poverty. This causing death, hunger and suffering. To date they have not fully recovered.

Cotton became the mainstay of the plantation system.

Senator James H. Hammond of South Carolina, in 1858 coined the famous phrase "Cotton is King." He was speaking in the United States Senate. "You dare not make war on cotton," he challenged. "No power on earth dares to make war on it." Cotton is King.

There was a saying in the golden years, "If the first crop of cotton makes you rich, what does the second crop make you?"

CHAPTER 1

Charleston, South Carolina was a major seaport town, it is on the east coast. A beautiful town, with enormous colonial homes that sit along the coast line. The streets are lined with large magnolia trees, apple blossoms and dog-wood trees.

On the waters edge sits large boats and ships that have made their way across the oceans, over the stormy seas, through the rough waters and rough times. They are waiting in rows along the docks to be unloaded and made ready for their return trip.

These are slave ships and the slaves have been brought in by the hundreds from the West Indies and Africa.

The cargo on these ships are waiting in eager anticipation for they did not know what to expect or what was waiting ahead for them.

The trip here was more than some of the slaves could endure and they never got to step foot on American soil. Others liked to think they would have been better off if they never had stepped on American soil.

They never forgot their home-land and customs, most of them were able to adjust to life as they knew it here but some were never able to accept this way of life.

In 1830, Charleston was a thriving, busy town. The slave market was very much in demand as was cotton.

The plantation owners had to have the slaves,

to produce the cotton that they grew on their plantations.

Instead of the ships returning empty, they would be loaded with bales of cotton. This cotton would be taken up north to the New England states or back across the sea to England.

Cotton was in such a demand that it was sold as fast as it could be produced.

England at this time would buy all the cotton that was available to them.

Cotton was king at this time and it made Charleston known for the rich, the arrogance, the slaves, and the cotton. It was also known for the poor whites.

Slaves were a very important link to cotton, because without the slaves, cotton could not have been raised economically.

Slavery had been a way of life in the south for over five generations.

As these slaves were taken from the ships they were put on the auction-blocks and sold to the plantation owners.

The plantation owners came from everywhere to buy these slaves. Some plantations owned a few but others would own in the hundreds.

Sometimes there was one single slave, at other times there would be two or more that would stay together and usually the buyer would buy all that came as a family. Other times they were split up and would be taken by different owners, never to see each other again.

With the slaves and cotton came another class. It was the "poor whites."

These whites most often were worse off than the slaves. The slaves were taken care of by their owners, but the whites had to provide for their own needs.

The slaves thought the poor whites were beneath them and they considered them lazy and "poor white trash."

Ray Crain, his wife Nancy, and daughter Martha had lived in Charleston all of their lives. He worked a small farm. Life was hard for him. With all the wealth in Charleston, it didn't seem as if it were for him.

Dreaming of a better life, he traded his small farm in Charleston for one hundred acres in Washington, Georgia, sight un-seen.

Washington was in North Georgia in the piedmont area, where the main crop grown was cotton.

He knew there had to be a better way of life and an easier way, so he knew this move must be his way to make it.

On April 1, 1840, Ray loaded his wife and daughter Martha, a rifle and very little else, except household goods in the wagon.

Hitching his two mules to the wagon, they left Charleston never to return. Ray had dreams of being a plantation owner.

Nancy had some reservations about this move as she had been brought up in a more protective environment.

But this was an exciting time for Ray and his family anyway, they knew things were not going to be easy but just thinking about what was ahead was enough excitement for them to want to go on. They knew the country would be different, with the trees and the growth of all that would be growing in North Georgia, it would be a big change to what they knew in Charleston.

The people would even be different. There was just a different way of life where they were going but it was what they wanted.

With a lot of hard work, a lot of determination, patience, and the guidance from the one above, they knew they could make it.

Ray was thirty years of age, red hair, six foot tall and weighing a hundred and ninety pounds. He was of Irish decent.

Nancy was also thirty years of age, five feet five inches tall and weighing a hundred fifteen pounds. She had black long hair and was of French decent.

Martha was six years old, black long hair and blue eyes, olive complexion. She was a very pretty child.

CHAPTER 2

They started on their journey about daylight. The roads were rough and riding in the wagon was not easy.

Sometimes Nancy and Martha would walk along side the wagon, they were able to pick flowers and sometimes they would find some wild berries that were growing along the road. They stopped and picked these as they could have them to eat with their supper.

Sometimes they passed an old home place that was deserted. The house was in shambles so they knew no one had lived there for some time.

Ray would often stop the wagon and they would rest for awhile. They might even find an old apple tree that was heavy with fruit. This would please Martha very much because she was able to pick the apples and put them in the wagon. Before long they were ready to go on because they knew there would be something new on up the road waiting for them.

The first day they were only able to go about ten miles. This seemed like a long ways to Nancy. This was hard going and you had to adjust to it all.

The first night they stopped a little earlier than they probably would at other times because they came to a creek and the water was so clear and beautiful and so abundant. They were very tired and thirsty and they knew it would be very nice to take a bath in the warm water.

Ray also knew that his mules would have plenty of grass and water by stopping here.

They stopped in plenty of time before it got dark because they had to gather wood for a fire and cook their meal and still have a little time to relax.

Ray un-hitched the mules from the wagon so they could eat and browse around some.

As he was setting up camp and busy with the chores, he heard the baying of hounds in the distance. He stopped and listened for a while, as this was a familiar sound to him, as he had heard it many times where he came from, but it usually meant someone was in trouble.

This trouble could mean that a slave had run-a-way and the dogs were on his track. Usually the run-a-way would not be able to get far because every one knew when a slave was on the run, and most times he was unable to get help.

Ray listened to the sounds for a minute, then he asked Nancy, "Do you know what that sound is?" He said, "Someone is tracking a run-a-way slave."

He thought to himself, I wonder why he is running away, probably there is a good reason.

As he was talking to Nancy, he heard a noise coming from the bushes, he turned, and as he did he saw a negro that was partly hidden in the brush. Then the negro came over to where they were and Ray knew he was a slave.

The slave had been trying to hide all along the way as he was scratched and torn and very tired looking.

This startled Ray and Nancy as they did not know what could be following him. Ray reached for his gun, which he always kept close at hand, because he was not sure what might happen next.

The slave began talking to Ray and was trying to tell him what had happened, and at the same time was begging Ray to help him. He knew without help he could not go much further. He knew the hounds were getting closer by their sounds. He also knew they did not give up easily.

Ray knew that if anyone was caught helping or hindering the capture of a slave that they would automatically be prosecuted.

Ray knew what would happen to the slave if he did not get help, he thought about this for a minute and knew that by helping the slave he had nothing to loose and anyway he didn't want to see him mistreated.

Ray picked up a can of coal-oil that was sitting under the wagon, he kept this for starting camp fires. This coal-oil has a very strong smell and burns quick so it doesn't take very much when it is used. Ray had the can in his hand and he motioned for the slave to follow him to the creek.

The creek was about one hundred feet away from the wagon where they made camp.

Standing on the bank of the creek by the stream, he poured the coal-oil on the feet of the slave. This was to kill the scent and it would throw the dogs off the track of the slave and would give him more time to get away.

The creek was flowing east. Ray told the slave to throw his coat in the water, hoping that by doing this the current would carry it down stream and possibly it would catch on the brush in the water. Whoever was chasing the slave would think he was in the water and this would throw him off track.

The slave had not gotten in the water but was running along the bank of the creek and he was going west. With the coal-oil on his feet he was hoping the dogs would loose his scent.

Ray figured he would never see the slave again because he had no reason to stay around and that was fine with him, because he only wanted to help him escape.

Very little time had passed and just as Ray was returning to the wagon, the dogs came running into camp. There were about ten in the pack.

These dogs were so mean looking that anyone who was being chased would try to get away and would be in fear of their lives. Ray knew what the dogs would do when they caught whatever it was they were chasing. Whether it was a slave or an animal.

Ray told himself he was glad he had helped the slave.

The dogs were able to take the scent to the creek but that is as far as they could go with it. They would run up and down sniffing, back and forth and around but could not pick it up again. The dogs were totally confused and didn't know which way to go.

This gave the slave more time to get further up the creek, with the coal-oil on his feet it was impossible for the dogs to track him any further.

By now the dogs were in a panic, not knowing which way to go or what to do, they became more excited and started fighting each other.

Ray had returned to the camp, he was thinking he had done a good deed as he had befriended the slave and he felt good about what he had done because he needed all the help he could get.

He started back to his chores as it was late and he didn't want it to get dark before he finished.

He was having good thoughts about the slave being able to get away from dogs, when all of a sudden he was startled again by someone coming through the brush. He looked and knew immediately that it was a patroler and knew what he was after.

The patroler was looking for the slave and he didn't care what he had to do to catch him, just as long as he did. He was as mean looking as his dogs, guess he had been around them so long that he was beginning to look and act like them. He was called "Mean Marvin."

Ray knew this patroler when he lived in Charleston. He made his living from the bounty that was offered by catching run-a-way slaves.

Mean Marvin was riding a big horse. The horse was so prancy that Marvin could hardly hold him. He was carrying a big long shot gun, chains, rope and a whip. He knew the dogs were not far ahead and he also knew by the sound and the way they were acting, that he had to be close on the track of the slave.

He knew he would be catching him very soon, he was almost always able to get what he was chasing. But little did he know this time would be different. The slave had been helped and was running as fast as he could go up stream.

The patroler talked to Ray for a short time and told him what he was looking for. Ray did not offer him much help and he did not say that he had even seen the slave, much less tell him he had helped him.

Quickly the patroler went to the creek where the dogs were and they were still snarling and fighting at each other. Seeing that the dogs were in utter confusion, he was angry and figured something had gone wrong.

Marvin was also confused about which way to go. He figured the slave had jumped in the creek, but which way did he go, up stream or down stream.

As he was trying to decide what to do, his eyes caught the glimpse of the slaves coat that was lodged on a snag about two hundred feet down stream, where the current had carried it.

Right off he thought the slave was going down stream and his coat had gotten caught on a snag. He was in such a hurry to get away, he just pulled out of the coat and left it on the snag.

Patrolers were known to be a hard bunch, and they were not easy to be misled, but this time the trick had worked. Marvin went for the bait, because he was so anxious to catch the slave he just could not give up. Marvin went down stream while the slave was going west up stream.

Marvin was getting anxious for he thought he was closing in, spurring his horse they went down stream hoping to find where the slave came out of the water.

As Marvin was riding along the creek bank he had pulled his "hog-leg" pistol out, he started firing at anything that he saw move hoping it might scare the slave out in the open but it only excited the dogs more.

Ray helped the slave escape because he knew the patrolers would be after him and he didn't think too highly of them, particularly this one, known as "Mean Marvin."

Ray remembered some of the things he had seen from the patrolers and the treatment they had given the slaves when they were caught.

He knew he had violated the law by helping the

slave escape, but he could not stand to see him get what he knew the patroler would do when he caught him. The slave had violated the law by running away.

The patrolers were known that when they would catch a run-a-way, rather than take him back to his owner, they would pretend he was never found and would take him to another plantation and sell him for more than the bounty that the owner would pay. It was easy for them to make false ownership papers.

The slaves were willing to go along with this because they could evade the punishment they were sure to get when they where returned to their owner, of course most of the time they had no choice, because the patroler was out to make all the money he could.

This run-a-way slave weighed about 180 pounds, was 5 feet 10 inches tall and about 40 years old. He was considered to be about in his prime.

Any owner of a plantation would be most willing to pay a good price for a slave of this caliber.

CHAPTER 3

Ray and his wife, Nancy, and Martha had settled down for the night. Hoping to get a good nights sleep as he had a long day ahead of him. The first day had been much more than they had expected.

He had hobbled his mules for the night down by the stream where there was plenty of grass and water.

They arose early the next morning as the sun was just coming up. Ray was feeling good that he had been able to help the slave but now it was time to get ready and move on his way.

They cooked their breakfast on the camp fire, Ray hitched the team to the wagon and they started out again on their trip to Georgia.

The weather was very nice this time of year, it was in the springtime and there was a little rain. The country side was covered with wild flowers and budding trees. Martha would pick flowers as she and her mother walked along side the wagon, and they would sing songs together.

After a few miles down the road, the slave they had helped the day before, came out of the bushes. Ray was very surprised to see him again but was glad to know the patroler had not found him.

The slave was keeping out of sight for he was afraid the patroler might return. He knew the patrolers did not give up easy.

He had walked through bushes, run a lot when the ground was flat and had not rested all night for fear the patroler would catch up to him.

The slave hadn't eaten for about three days. In his weaken condition he could hardly go any further. He knew that Ray would be coming this way in his wagon, and was hoping he would help him again.

As the slave approached the wagon, he said to Ray, "Massa, Massa, could you help me one more time? I am hungry and if I don't get some food I know I can't go on much further and the patroler will find me."

Ray said, "What the hell," he knew it was illegal to help a slave escape, but really in his own mind he knew that the slave needed help and thought to hell with the consequence.

The slave told Ray that the patroler had been chasing him for several days, and they did not give up if there was any hope left at all of finding him.

The reason the slave was running away, was his master had died and he was going to be sold. (Being sold was the biggest fear of any slave.) Ray knew that he was telling the truth because he had no reason to lie to him. It was beginning to seem to Ray that his destiny was to help this slave.

Nancy fixed him something to eat, and while he was eating he told Ray that his name was "Mo Green." He had been on the Green plantation all his life. His master, Massa Green had died and he could not stand to be sold to a new owner.

The patroler had seen the slave at different times while he was chasing him, but Mo had been able to evade the patroler by getting in a stream which would throw the dogs off his tracks.

Mo's shoes were just hanging on his feet, and his clothes were torn and very dirty. So Ray dressed him in some clean clothes that he had of his own. This way if anyone saw the slave with Ray they wouldn't be so quick to think that he did not belong to him if he was a little more presentable.

Ray and Mo were hoping by now that the patroler was gone for good.

Mo was asking Ray if he would let him go along with them to where they were going. He said he would work at whatever was to be done and he would not be a burden to him.

Mo knew he could not get far away on his own and he also knew Ray would need help where he was going.

Ray decided at this time to let Mo go along with them. He knew he would always need help when he got to his new land. They were both in trouble anyway with the law, Mo by running away from the plantation and Ray by helping him escape.

Ray told Mo that he could go with them but they still had to be careful of the patroler. Ray said he could hide in the wagon if the patroler was seen coming. They would pour coal-oil on his shoes again and Ray would pull off the road and Mo would have to run again and stay hidden. This was fine with Mo.

At this time a slave man in his prime was worth around four thousand dollars. This was a considerable loss for the plantation owner when he lost a slave.

This violation of the selling of the run-a-way slaves to other plantation owners made many patrolers wealthy.

CHAPTER 4

The second day on the road they were only able to travel about 10 miles. Traveling in the wagon didn't seem to get any easier. Late afternoon they started to make camp for another night and take care of the daily chores.

After they had cooked their dinner and eaten, Ray decided that he had better get rid of the old clothes that Mo had been wearing. Just in case the patroler came by he would not be able to find them. So Ray put them on the campfire and burnt them.

They settled down for the night. Ray, Nancy, and Martha slept inside the wagon and Mo slept under it on a bed he had made. Everything was peaceful.

The night was clear and a warm breeze was blowing through the trees. A scent of spring flowers could be smelled in the air.

Every now and then a coyote howl could be heard in the distance.

These four people were resting in their beds and they were wondering what the new day would bring for them as they knew they were riding to their destiny.

The next morning they arose early and Ray told Mo it would be near impossible for him to escape from the patroler by himself without help.

Ray told Mo he could go along with him to his new plot of land in Georgia.

Ray said he would have a better chance of not getting caught if he was with them.

Ray said there was a lot of hard work ahead for both of them.

They would be clearing the land, building the house and barns. They would have to learn to survive on their own in a new place.

Mo gladly accepted the invitation, knowing full well he might be caught anyway. So they both agreed that he should go.

Nancy was not too enthused about helping Mo escape but she did realize that they would need some extra help. So she went along with the plan. Martha was sorry for Mo as she knew he had no place to live and nothing to eat. She wanted to help him too.

Ray was talking to Mo and told him that in his past if he had murdered anyone or raped someone or had stolen any thing except food, that he would not help him anymore and that he would have to leave the wagon.

Mo said he was happy when he lived on the Green plantation until his master had died and he was going to be sold.

He had never done anything but work in the cotton fields. He was just a "field negro" and he would not hurt anyone.

Ray was satisfied with what Mo had said and told him that he could go on with them to Georgia. Ray would need his help.

They did have breaking the law in common. They also had in common "survival." More or less they were bound to each other.

Ray told Mo he could walk away at anytime and

nothing would be done about it.

The days that followed were about the same, nothing unusual happening. Just a few wagons passing, sometimes they would stop and talk a while but mostly they just raised a hand as they went by.

The Crains arrived at their destination in about two weeks.

During this time Ray and Mo had become well acquainted.

Mo was helping in every way he could, including getting wood for the fire, helping with the team and getting water when it was needed.

Mo was wondering all the while where the patroler was and for sure he was staying out of sight.

At night when they camped, Mo would tell Martha animal stories that he learned as a child when he was growing up on the Green plantation.

He also would make her dolls that he would whittle out of wood. Mo was very good with his hands. This made Mo and Martha feel close to each other.

Nancy was still in doubt about Mo and wondering what would happen to them if they were caught helping him escape. She also knew that they needed him and tried to put the thought out of her mind.

CHAPTER 5

Ray, Nancy, Martha and Mo finally arrived at their destination in Washington, Georgia.

They had been traveling for about 2 weeks. Some days the going was fine and other days it was pretty rough.

They had some trouble with the wagon and would have to stop and spend some time repairing it.

With help from the neighbors Ray was able to find his plot of land, which he had purchased before he left Charleston.

The plot of land consisted of 100 acres. The land was mostly covered with pine trees and brush.

With ax and saw, Ray and Mo started work clearing the land of trees. These were needed to build the house and barns. They worked from sun up until sun down.

In the meantime they had to live in the wagon until they could get enough logs to build the house. But sometimes when the weather was real nice, they just slept outside.

It didn't take too long to build a two room house, they were happy just to have this for a start even if it was small.

Mo lived in the wagon until they could get his cabin built.

Game was plentiful in the area and all around, so they had plenty to eat because Ray was a good marksman.

On the south side of the property the closest

neighbors were about a mile and half away. They were the Boggs family. Tom Boggs and his two sons, Frank and Jeff. They were about 22 and 25 years old. They were a rough looking pair, English descent, 6 foot, 200 pounds, sandy hair. Jeff the oldest.

The boys never saw the inside of a school house and didn't figure they needed to read or write because they were not going anywhere anyway. But they were expert shots with a rifle.

Their life was about as free as anyone could want. They hunted with their dogs and would do some trapping of various animals. This was only so they could have a little extra money from selling the hides.

The Boggs land was a ten acre plot and the boys would do a little farming only when their daddy made them. That was enough land for them because they didn't require much.

They also worked at different farms for extra cash. They would use the money to buy supplies to furnish their liquor still. They made the liquor for Tom and to sell. The boys didn't drink, they were good solid boys.

Their mother had died two years before and was buried back of the house. She died from hard work and exposure.

On the north side of the property was the Peteet plantation.

The Peteet plantation was big and there was over a 100 slaves on the place. William Peteet was known as a planter.

The Peteet plantation expressed wealth. Two story, beautiful elaborate house with four white columns in front, balcony above the front door, bell tower on top which was rung at noon time and evening for the slaves to come in from the fields.

Inside was a long winding staircase, beautiful crystal chandeliers hanging in every room. Carved wainscotting was on the walls, this was made from solid walnut wood and hand carved with designs of animals and horse drawn chariots. This carving was done by the slaves in the winter time when they could not work in the fields.

A porch on the front of the house that went almost around on every side. There was a long beautiful winding driveway leading up to the front door.

The plantation was the very heart of the south. High productions of cotton and cheap labor.

Ray and Mo continued with their work of clearing the land, building a cabin for Mo and building the barns.

Ray had bought a cow from Tom Boggs so they could have milk and butter, and Nancy would be able to bake some for them now.

The land where they had cleared was now used for a garden. So things were beginning to ease up a little for them now.

Mo put a rail fence around the garden, as the deer were very prevalent around there.

They continued to clear the land as they needed to put to use all they had. They needed to get a crop of cotton planted because that was one reason they came to this part of the country. This land was good for growing cotton, but their cash also was running out.

The Boggs boys were a lot of help to Ray and Mo. They also brought some vegetables from their garden and they would use their horses to help them clear the land. They were a rough looking bunch, but really were good boys.

Tom Boggs never lifted a finger to help out but he sure could ride hard on the boys and their dogs. He also could curse more in less time than Ray had ever heard from anyone, and he had surely heard a lot, as he was from Charleston.

All the rough talk that Tom Boggs did was just a cover up to keep the boys in line and most times they needed it. But Jeff and Frank would act like they never heard a word their daddy said but they knew better than not to do what he said.

The Boggs took for granted that Mo was Ray's own slave-hand and never asked anything about it. They really didn't care one way or the other.

They were happy with their life the way it was. Without much stress or worry.

CHAPTER 6

The work continued on the farm from sun up until sun-down.

The Boggs boys just helped spasmodically because they could not stand any kind of work regularly.

They told Ray about the Alabama Creek Indians. They said he would be in jeopardy because he did not have any dogs to protect his home.

Ray knew about the Indians and their raids but he thought that had been over a long time ago. Ray was not too concerned.

The Creek Indians were bitter because they had been cheated out of their land when they were in Georgia. That is why they had to move on to Alabama.

Periodically the Indians came back to Georgia to raid and steal. This was mostly from hatred and not from hunger. But if anything got in their way they would kill, sometimes they didn't have to be progged into it. The Indians did't consider who was responsible for their plight, they just knew it was the white man who had taken their land and they would never be happy. They just wanted revenge.

Tom Boggs and his family had settled on their plot of land about ten years ago. They were what was referred to as the "poor whites," sometimes known as the "poor white trash," by some plantation owners.

Tom had a few cattle, hogs and some chickens. This was enough to keep them going as it was all he wanted. This was one reason they were called poor whites.

The social standing of the slaves was the house negro, he was number one.

The field negro was the lowest, but he had no desire to change his status because he had grown up with his family and friends, and he did not want to leave them.

Even though they did not have access to the big house, they still felt they were part of the plantation.

The house negro was lighter in color and worked in the Big House. This made him feel more important than a field negro.

The field negro which was most important of all to the plantation, because without him the work could not have been done.

The field negro looked at the "poor whites" as lower than he was.

It was mid summer. Ray and Mo had been able to put in about ten acres of cotton.

Ray had gone to Washington several times for supplies. The money by now was really getting low.

Ray and Mo remembered what the Boggs boys had told them. The boys said they could make extra money by working at the Peteet plantation. The owner William Peteet had over a 100 slaves but he needed all the help he could get. Especially someone that could do something extra good. He hired by the day.

Taking a chance that Mo might be recognized as a run-a-way, they put that fear behind them and went over to talk to the owner, William Peteet.

They decided they had to take a chance to get

extra money,

Ray and Mo went to see Massa William. He was a tall, grayish haired man, about 150 pounds. In his fifties, single, and very distinguished looking.

There was a negro mammy in charge of the Big House. She had been at the plantation for years and worked always in the Big House.

She was well aware of everything that went on and nothing got by her.

Mammy weighed about 300 pounds and was 5 feet 5 inches. She was proud of her job and certainly took charge.

Massa William hired Mo and he was to begin work the next day in the fields. When it came time for Mo to go to work in the morning, it was raining.

When Mo got to the plantation they had him start work in the black smith shop. Not knowing that he was a master craftsman.

As Mo worked in the shop the first day, he was able to repair things that had been broken for years. Massa William had not been able to find anyone before with the skills that Mo had. He did such a good job and they were so pleased with his work that he decided to let him stay in the shop and work instead of sending him out to the fields.

Mo was not only good at forging iron and steel, but was also very good with wood. It seemed there was nothing he could not fix or repair in the shop.

Massa William wanted Mo to stay at the plantation, but Mo would not leave Ray. He had done so much for him.

CHAPTER 7

Mammy had several girls helping her in the Big House. She was very particular so she required a lot of help.

The first day that Mo was there working in the black smith shop, Mammy noticed one of her girls, her name was Ring, could not stay away from the shop. She was always going back and forth to see if she could get Mo a drink or something to eat.

The overseer of the plantation was Briarfield, a white man. He had a wife and two daughters. They lived in a house close to the Big House. He was in charge of the fields and black smith shop.

After Briarfield saw what Mo could do in the shop, he was completely sold on his ability. He wanted him to continue work as long as possible.

When Mo finished a days work he would take his wages and go home to the Crain farm. He continued to work at the Peteet plantation for several weeks, fixing what ever needed fixing.

He was getting a sizable amount of money and he gave it to the Crain farm.

Mammy continued to watch Ring and Mo, and they continued to laugh and talk and get more friendly.

Mammy tells Ring, "You quit bellying-up to him. You know nothing about him and you could git yourself in trouble."

He could be as low-down and sorry as poor white trash, but this did not stop Ring and Mo from carrying on.

Back in Charleston, the patroler felt he had been out-witted and was bitter.

The Green plantation where Mo had run-away from, had been left to the heirs.

The patroler found out that the Green's had freed all their slaves. Mean Marvin was informed that Mo was not wanted as a run-a-way anymore.

Ole Marvin, with his ego hurt, was not satisfied with this. He figured the only thing that Mo could have done was go to Washington, and the only way he could have done that is someone had to help him get away.

The patroler thought if Mo had continued to go down the creek, he would have come out in Charleston.

Ole Marvin knew he wasn't in Charleston, so he had figured Mo did not know he had been freed. As he would not have been talking to anyone that would have known.

So Ole Marvin might be able to get Mo after all and sell him to another plantation. As he already had false papers of his ownership.

Marvin goes to Washington and it was no time until he found there was black man that fit Mo's description.

He knew he was hot on the trail again. His horse had developed a limp by this time, so he had to rent one from the livery stable. The horse he rented was wild and about half broken. This was unknown to him at the time. He was in such a hurry to get on Mo's trail, he probably wouldn't have cared anyway about the horse.

In no time he arrived at the Peteet plantation and he finally found where Mo was.

So waiting until the next day, he made his move on the Crain farm.

He caught Mo un-aware going to the barn. He leveled his gun at him and climbed off his horse and shackled him.

He had put the shackles on Mo and climbed back on his horse, when a covey of quails was startled when Mo stepped back off the trail and flushed them. They made such a noise that Marvin's horse started bucking and running. This throwing Marvin off the horse and one foot got tangled in the chains that were on the saddle. The horse started dragging him through the woods.

Marvin was hollering as loud as he could by this time.

Ray hearing the commotion, started running after the horse. The horse still dragging Marvin and going at a full run.

The horse dragged Marvin for about two miles. The horse was out of breath and had gotten tangled in some vines. Ray finally was able to get to him. Marvins foot was still caught in the chains on the saddle.

He was badly hurt. Ray releasing Marvin from the horse and leaving him lying on the ground, he left Mo to stay with him while he went to get Dr. Wise.

The horse went galloping back to the livery

stable dragging the chains.

Marvin was carried to Washington on a stretcher and Dr. Wise informed him that he was going to die soon. Marvin did not want to die with this on his conscious. So he told the sheriff how he had been trying to find Mo, and that he had planned to sell him to another plantation owner. He told the sheriff he knew Mo had been freed but Mo did not know it, so therefore it would have been easy to sell him to a new owner.

The sheriff hearing this, freed Mo and Ray of all charges.

Soon after this statement, Marvin died. It is ironic that the chains he used to bind the slaves was also instrumental in his death.

Mo went back to work at the Peteet plantation in the black smith shop.

Ring knowing he was there, she could not stay away from the shop.

Mammy was getting madder by the minutes. She was in charge of everything that happens in the Big House and her word was law.

Overseer Briarfield was in charge of the fields and his word was law over the field hands.

There were two slaves that were put in charge of the grounds around the Big House. They were born with poor health and were too weak to work in the fields.

One was named Pockets, because he kept his hands in his pockets most of the time. The other one was named Stovepipe, he was tall, slender, with a smoky like complexion.

Pockets was short and little. They had been born on the plantation, but they were limited to what they could do, both physically and mentally. Mammy rode hard on them continually.

Mammy was worked hard keeping up with everything in the Big House.

She had Stovepipe and Pockets that had to be supervised in everything they did.

Massa William had a field hand about the age of Stovepipe and Pockets. He was too weak for hard work in the fields, but he learned quickly. His name was Willie. His friends would call him "Piss Willie," because when he was little his behind was always wet.

He was a big help to Mammy. She would allow no one to call him Piss Willie, saying "We are quality folks and not poor white trash." Although Willie did not mind the name.

Mammy claimed all her blacks as her own children. She loved them all and continued to help them whenever she could.

When they would get out of line, this fifty year old, three hundred pound, black woman, would set them straight quick. She would say, "I love all of you and we are quality folks ourselves and that's a fact."

Briarfield would take his oldest slaves and put them in charge of groups of ten to twenty men or more. At the end of the day, the slaves that were in charge reported to him. He then reported to the owner.

CHAPTER 8

Early one morning, Mo had gone to the Peteet plantation to work. Ray had gone to the field to work his crops.

Nancy was working in the house and she noticed someone coming up the road. The closer he got to the house, she could tell it was an Indian.

Martha was helping her mother in the house. Through instinct, she bolted the front door.

The Indian slowly came toward the cabin. He came to the front door and lifted the latch. When he found the door was locked, and he was unable to get in, he hollered, "Let me in."

Nancy told him to go away, she said my husband will be here any minute.

They presumed the Indian had been watching the cabin.

When the Indian could not get the door open, he lunged against it but the door would not come open. Nancy told Martha to hide under the bed. Nancy, knowing that she must do something quick, picked up the rifle that was used to kill game.

She had never fired a gun of any kind but she had to do it now. She was frightened out of her witts.

When the Indian decided that he could not break the door down, he went around to the side window and took his foot and pushed the window in.

He started to climb inside and as he was putting his leg through the hole, Nancy aimed the gun and pulled the trigger. The bullet glazed him on the side of the head, knocking him back out the window.

Bleeding profusely, he ran staggering towards the woods.

Nancy and Martha were beside themselves with fear.

She dropped the rifle and they both ran as fast as they could go toward the field where Ray was working.

Ray had heard the gun shot and was already starting toward the cabin.

Beside herself with fear, Nancy could hardly talk, but Ray could get the drift of what had happened.

Ray, Nancy and Martha ran to the Boggs house, which was about a mile and half away. Ray told them what had happened. The Boggs boys got their dogs and they started tracking the wounded Indian.

The dogs immediately picked up the track that went into the woods. Ray, Jeff, and Frank were following close behind the dogs.

The Indian found a stream and was wading in it, causing the dogs to lose his scent.

Darkness had set in and they decided to go home and continue tracking in the morning.

It had started to rain and rained all night. This made it impossible to track the Indian any further.

They knew that Nancy had hit him when she fired the gun because they found blood traces on the ground when they were tracking him.

He could already be dead for all they knew.

Nancy and Martha were still so afraid that Ray could not return to the fields for several days.

Tom Boggs, the boys daddy, never did any work, just curse and brag.

When they came back without the Indian, he said, "If I had been there tracking him you would have caught that damn Indian."

CHAPTER 9

Ray, Nancy, Martha, and Mo had been on their farm for about three years.

Mo was working on the Peteet plantation and Ray was still clearing the land and doing some farming.

They began to have a little extra money by now.

Nancy was still upset about having the incident with the Indian. Even though it had been three years she was still wondering if she had killed him or would he return.

Ray and Mo had barred the windows of the cabin to help Nancy feel more at ease when she was alone.

Nancy and Martha were still not too comfortable about being out-door unless Ray or Mo was home.

It was August and the weather was pretty hot.

Tom Boggs was sitting on his front porch, with his jug by his side, while the two boys had gone hunting taking the dogs.

Tom looked down the path that went by the house and he saw a big white dog coming. The dog had a muzzle hanging to one side of his mouth, it was almost torn from his neck as he had been fighting, and he was dragging a ten foot rope. Coming from his mouth was white foam.

Old Tom knew it was a mad dog. Tom had no gun at home, as the boys had taken them on the hunting trip.

So all he could do was follow at a good distance behind the dog and holler, "Mad dog, mad dog." By doing this he could warn anyone that might be coming down the path.

The dog was following the trail which led to the Crain property. The trail ran by the house and the barn. (It was about a 100 feet from the house to the barn.)

Martha was mid way on the trail, she was carrying a bucket of feed as she was helping with the feeding of the chickens.

Hearing Tom hollering "Mad dog, mad dog," she saw the dog coming straight at her. She was so scared she could not move.

Mo was coming in from working at the Peteet plantation. Seeing the situation, he ran toward Martha and literally picking her up, he sat her on the limb of a tree that was hanging over the trail. It was about six feet high, he had to hold her on the limb as she would have fallen off.

As Mo was standing under the tree, holding her on the limb, the dog kept coming straight at him, a mad dog only goes in a straight line, does not look to either side. The dog bit him on the leg and just went on toward the barn.

Ray was in the barn working and hearing the commotion, grabbed the ax. As he came out of the barn he met the dog head on. He hit him with one swing of the ax, killing him instantly.

Mo, sitting Martha on the ground, she ran back to the house, crying and scared.

Mo and Ray standing there looking at the dog and looking at each other, momentarily stunned, they were thinking about what had happened.

Ray asked Mo if the dog had bitten him and Mo answered yes. Pulling his pants leg up, he showed him the bite marks and where the skin was broken on his leg from the dog bite.

Ray told Mo to sit on the bench under the tree. He went to the big house for help.

When he arrived at the big house he told Massa William what had happened. Massa William immediately sent for Dr. Wise.

Ray returned to Mo to comfort him and it seemed like an eternity before the doctor came.

Dr. Wise cleaned the wound from the bite and bandaged it up.

The doctor took a sample of the saliva and sent it to Charleston to have it analyzed.

Dr. Wise was sure it was rabies but had to wait for the results of the test.

Calling Ray and Nancy aside, Dr. Wise told them he was almost sure what the results would be. Chances were that Mo would be dead before the analysis came back.

He told Ray and Nancy what they could expect from the bite.

He told them the incubation period for a rabies bite was about twenty-one days and it was almost always fatal. First, pain would appear around the bite area and trying to drink will become extremely painful. Then he will refuse to drink at all.

Next, a restless behavior is noticeable. Spasms and excitable are present. Convulsions occur, large amounts of thick saliva are present at the mouth.

Once the symptoms have appeared, death is almost inevitable in about two to three days, due to generalized paralysis.

Dr. Wise said he didn't feel Mo was ready to hear the results yet. He said he would check on him daily.

Mo was able to work a few more days at the black smith shop. All the negros were afraid to come in contact with him. As the days passed, Mo's condition became rapidly worse and the symptoms that Dr. Wise had told them about began to appear.

Mo and Ray boarded up the windows on Mo's cabin and took everything out that would cause him to get hurt on, except his bed.

Nancy had always cooked for Mo. Ray sawed a hole in the floor for Mo to use for personal use. Once he was stricken he would be unable to go outside to use the outhouse which was in back of his cabin.

There was nothing that Ray and Nancy could do but watch and observe him and try to keep him from getting hurt.

A hole was also cut in the door to pass his food through. Martha passed the door crying, being sorry for Mo and putting the blame on herself for him being bitten.

She had a great love for Mo and he did also for her.

Ring, his girl-friend, visited him daily until he died.

Mammy did not rare at her anymore. Everyone

was sad. Nancy took good care of Mo since they had helped him escape.

This was a sad ending for this negro that had been a slave for forty years at the Green plantation.

Finally he was free and was coming into his own. Mo didn't seem to worry, but he was very quiet.

He would sit under the tree for hours, at times he could go out to the fields to help Ray. Even before the rabies struck him, he seemed to have various moods. He was feeling out of place in whatever he did.

Martha was refusing to eat and was crying a lot, continuing putting the blame on herself. They kept her feelings from Mo because everyone was feeling sad for Mo.

Massa William made frequent visits to see Mo, promising him if there was anyway to heal him, no matter what the cost was, he would take care of it. He checked daily to see if he could do anything for him.

On the twentieth day, Mo voluntarily went into the cabin to be locked in, as his symptoms began to appear and Mo asked to be locked in the cabin.

Pain had already started at the bite and trying to drink was extremely painful for him. Then he refused to drink at all and he was behaving very peculiar. He was very excitable and begging Ray to shoot him to stop his suffering.

On the twenty-first day he began having spasms and convulsions occurred. A large amount of thick saliva appeared.

Mo was dead on the twenty-fourth day. This was almost too much for the Crain family to bear.

He was buried at the back of his cabin on the farm. Nancy read from the bible about a good shepherd,

Martha still feeling it was her fault, she did not want to play anymore with the dolls that he had made for her.

CHAPTER 10

Mo had been dead three years now and the farm was prospering and everyone was back to near normal again.

The far side of the farm had never been cleared of timber. Ray would go there to work and he would stay as late as he could see to work. He wanted to use the new ground for spring planting.

It was getting late in the evening and was time for Ray to come home for supper. Nancy had supper ready and waiting for him to come in. She became concerned because he was later than usual coming in. She sent Martha to the field to tell her daddy to come in.

The sun had begun to set and as Martha got close to where her daddy had been working, she called to him but she did not get any answer. This made her anxious.

As she got closer she could see that the team of mules had gotten tangled in some bushes and as she walked closer to them she looked down and saw her daddy lying face down on the ground and he had an arrow sticking in his back. His head was covered with blood.

Gathering her courage, she knew what she had to do. She had to walk a mile and half through the woods to the Boggs farm, wondering all the time if the killer was around.

As she was running through the woods, even the shadows in the trees seem to reach out to her.

Nancy was still waiting back at the house for Martha and her daddy to come in, becoming more anxious all the time.

When Martha arrived at the Boggs house, fear had gripped her so bad she could hardly talk.

Jeff and Frank listened as she was trying to tell them what had happened. Calling to their dogs and getting their rifles, they started out to the field.

When they got to the field where Ray was lying, seeing there was nothing they could do for him. They untangled the mules so they could go back to the barn.

The arrow that Ray was shot with had gone completely through his body and the blood that Martha saw on his head was because he was half scalped.

It was believed that the killer became frightened when Martha was calling to her daddy and he ran off.

Rays pocket watch and knife were missing. Jeff and Frank, with their dogs picked up a track that was leaving the field, going into the woods.

They knew it was a fresh track by the way the dogs were barking and the speed they were running. Jeff and Frank could hardly keep up with the dogs.

Tom Boggs walked Martha back to her house, and informed Nancy what had happened. Tom then went to Washington for the sheriff.

The moon was full and it was bright as day. The Boggs boys with their dogs and lanterns had the Indian caught in less than an hour.

The dogs had surrounded him and he could not

go any further.

Jeff and Frank searched him and found Ray's watch and pocket knife in his pouch.

Keeping a rifle at his head as they started taking him back to the place where Ray was found, the Indian spooked and started to run.

Jeff told his lead dog to "get him." The Indian was not able to go but a few feet until the dog had downed him. Reaching in one of his leggins, the Indian pulled out a six inch knife and stabbed the dog in the throat.

Jeff taking aim, put a bullet through his heart.

By this time Tom Boggs had returned with the sheriff and posse.

Frank and the dogs were with the dead Indian while Jeff was talking to the sheriff and posse. When the sheriff heard their story about what had happened, he draped the Indian over a horse and took him to Washington.

As the sheriff was examining the Indian, he pulled back his hair and on the left side of his head he found a scar about a half inch wide and about four inches long. He said, "I believe this is the same Indian that Nancy had shot several years ago."

Showing Nancy the body she said it was.

She said, "If I hadn't been such a bad shot, my husband would still be living." With this she completely broke down.

The next day Ray was buried along side of Mo. Nancy read a verse from the bible over Ray saying, "Lord take these evil things away from us." After this the Boggs boys buried Ray.

Hearing about this, Massa William went to the Crain farm. Telling Nancy that she and Martha should not stay there by themselves. They should come with him and stay in the big house until something could be worked out.

The Boggs boys were taking care of the animals and stock.

In a few days Massa William offered to buy the Crain farm and told Nancy and Martha they could stay in the big house as long as they wanted to.

The price that Massa William offered her for the farm was much more than it was worth. Nancy realized this, she knew she couldn't live there so she said yes to his offer.

She had kept records and did all the bookkeeping at their farm, so she was able to help out on the plantation. In time she was able to take care of all the books at the plantation.

Martha would help and supervise in the nursery of the pick-a-ninnies while their mothers were working.

CHAPTER 11

Ten years had passed. Martha had blossomed into a beautiful woman. She was tall, slender and very elegant looking, with long black hair and beautiful olive complexion. Her manner was very dainty, she had gotten this training from her mother that had been reared in a prominent family from Charleston.

Martha was raised as an only child, so this gave her confidence in herself.

Martha and Nancy still carried a guilt feeling in their hearts of what had happened years before and could not dismiss it.

Martha's guilt was, "If I had not of frozen in the trail, Mo would still be alive."

Nancy's feeling was, "If I had been a better shot with the gun and killed the Indian, Ray would still be alive."

These feelings haunted them both. Time went by and Nancy could not cope with the guilt feeling and the loneliness of missing Ray. She became frail and thin.

As days passed, she was confined to her bed. She asked to be moved to a room with a window facing the field. She wanted to hear the singing of the darkies as they did their work in the fields. She loved to hear them singing and they always sang as they worked.

Three days later she died as she was listening to the singing.

Nancy was buried on the farm along side of Ray and Mo.

Dr. Wise came by daily to see her while she was sick, in her passing he said she died from a bad heart, but it was really from a broken heart.

Martha took this very hard, with all that had happened, she knew life must still go on. She had endured more in her life in a short time than most people ever know. But this had made her stronger and therefore she was capable of handling things that were necessary for her to do.

Mammy was sad and very quiet. She said she knew someone was going to die, because she had heard a dog howling through the night. This was supposed to be a bad omen through their thinking.

Massa William had been noticing Martha now for some time.

Even though there was a wide age span between them, this did not bother William, and Martha had not ever given it a thought.

She had learned to respect him as he was always there when trouble came to any of them, and was always ready to help.

William knew that Martha was thinking about what she must do now, all the people she had loved were gone and she was left alone.

William assured her that she would not have to leave the plantation and he was willing to do whatever he could to make her happy again.

CHAPTER 12

A year had passed and things were going as usual with the help of everyone.

William and Martha had become very close friends. She had no one else that she could talk to or depend on. He had wanted her to know that she could depend on him for anything she might need and it gave him great pleasure when she did come to him for something.

He told her that he had never been married and would like to have an heir to his plantation.

He told her that she had been there long enough and knew the way the plantation was run.

He also told her he did care for her, he knew he wasn't getting any younger and if she would marry him, he would be very happy for her to be his wife.

She told him that she respected him and that she liked living on the plantation. She said in time she knew she could love him, but she wanted some time to think about it before she gave him an answer.

Martha thought about what Massa William had asked her, she knew she did care for him and she was happy living on the plantation.

It made her feel very special that he would consider her to be his wife. She knew that he was a very eligible man and that many pretty girls were always after him, but she kept wondering if she could live up to what he needed in a wife.

After several days of thinking about what William had asked her and all the time he was trying to win her confidence, she said yes to him, and told him she would be happy to be his wife.

Things started happening, plans were being made for the wedding and everyone in the big house was very excited about Massa William and Martha getting married. They all loved her as she was a lovable person and she was kind to everyone she came in contact with.

Invitations were made and were sent to all their friends, to every plantation far and wide.

William had several occasions where he could have gotten married, but he never found anyone before that he thought would be satisfactory to be his wife.

William wanted everyone to be there so Martha could be introduced to his friends as his wife.

Mammy and all the girls and the outside help were getting the house and the grounds ready for the big celebration. Food of every kind was being prepared and brought in as it was going to be the biggest event of the year.

Martha was very excited. She kept thinking to herself how proud her mother and daddy would be if they could be here and share in this occasion with her.

She traveled to Savannah to get her wedding dress and whatever else she might want or need.

She spent several days in Savannah shopping and just looking at all the beautiful clothes. she wondered if she would be able to fit in with the other women of the plantations, but she really didn't care whether she did or not. She just wanted to be a good wife to Massa William.

The day finally came when she was going to be Mrs. William Rabun Peteet.

She arose very early that morning, because she had a lot of preparation to do to get ready for the wedding of the year, and anyway she was too excited to stay in bed any longer.

With the help of Mammy and Ring, (Ring was given to her as her own personal maid), she was ready.

The house and grounds were filled with friends that had come from far and near. They were all very happy for William, as he had been a good friend and neighbor. They all knew Martha would be a good wife for him.

Martha was very beautiful, William thought she was the most beautiful girl he had every seen. She glowed with radiance. As she slowly came down the stairs and stood by the side of William, you could feel the presence of love in the air that these two people had for each other.

As all their friends looked on and their personal help was there, you could see a tear in their eye occasionally. They were not sad tears but tears of joy for Martha and William. Everyone was so happy for them both.

That day they became Mr. and Mrs. William Rabun Peteet. There was a party that surpassed all expectations. Everyone danced, ate, drank and had a wonderful time until late in the night.

William gave Martha a beautiful honeymoon that

she could never forget, and it lasted until the day he died. They were very, very, happy, but the memory of it all stayed with her for the rest of her life.

CHAPTER 13

About a year had passed since Martha and William had married, they were as happy as they knew they would be.

William continued in the same routine that he had always done of running the plantation. It required him to be away from home a lot of the time.

Martha realized that this was necessary and she did not object to it. She knew what was needed to handle things on the plantation, and there was always plenty of help for her.

Sometimes the trips would take him to Savannah, sometimes to Charleston and then there was Atlanta. Martha never questioned his where-abouts or why he had stayed so long. She was happy with what she was doing and what was required of her, that she thought these trips were necessary for him to take, anyway she was in love and nothing else mattered.

Martha was now about four months pregnant. William and Martha were very happy about this and were looking forward to the coming event, of course this brought him to be more attentive to Martha and to please her in whatever way possible. He was now going to have the heir to his plantation that he had so wanted.

William was away on a trip. He had been gone for several days, Martha knew this was not uncommon for him to be away for periods at a time, but this time it seemed to be different. She had an uneasy feeling about him being gone. He was in Charleston and suddenly he became very sick. He was immediately taken to the hospital in Charleston and doctors worked with him intensively, but there was nothing they could do for him, he died suddenly. It was believed he had dissipated.

He was brought back to the plantation to be buried at home. Martha gave him a honorable funeral.

In a very short time, Martha became the owner of the Peteet plantation. It consisted of twelve hundred acres and over a hundred slaves.

The responsibility of the ownership of such a large plantation was enormous, but Martha went about the duties with great courage. She was very young to have this responsibility on her but Martha had been through many difficulties in her life and she would be able to handle this one also. She had the help and support of Mammy and all the hands on the plantation.

Things stayed about the same and were going very well. The negros in the fields did their jobs as usual and the house negros were supervised by Mammy and they knew what they were to do. Everyone tried to help the best they could, so there was little need for much change.

The first rule that Martha did make was there would be no whipping of any of the slaves. She found other ways of punishing if necessary.

Things moved smoothly and Martha's time was getting close, of course Mammy was taking care of her every needs and saw that she wanted for nothing.

Dr. Wise told her she probably would have no trouble in delivery.

It was time for her to give birth and she had a beautiful big, fine boy. She had an easy birth and Dr. Wise was happy the way things had gone.

She named the boy "Rabun Hood Peteet." It was another big day on the plantation, as everyone celebrated.

Martha was sad only because William could not be with her to share in her happiness. The boy was such a beautiful baby and he had many of his fathers features.

CHAPTER 14

It was now springtime at the plantation and planting of cotton was near. There was also corn to plant and a garden to make. They needed to have these fresh vegetables for the dinners in the big house.

This was a time of anticipation and everyone was looking forward to a bountiful crop. Acres and acres of cotton was planted and also acres of corn because they had to have the feed for the stock.

Summer came and passed rather quickly, the fall of the year was here and it was harvest time again.

This was an exciting time for everyone on the plantation. When it was cotton picking time things seemed to happen on the plantation. People were coming and going all the time, big machines were brought in to take the cotton to the cotton gins and then the cotton was baled and sent on to Charleston to be put on ships.

Later when things were all settled down again, new slaves were bought and some might be traded. This seemed to be a normal life for them.

Pockets was working in the yard when he saw a big carriage pulling in the circle drive in front of the house. He thought this was the biggest and finest carriage he had ever seen, with all its shiny brass, leather harness and big shiny wheels. There were two big beautiful horses pulling the carriage.

The driver also was very elegant looking and very fancy dressed in all the finery that a chauffer would wear. As he stepped down from the carriage he stated to Pockets that they wanted to see the lady of the house.

This pleased Pockets greatly as he was asked to do something special, he was excited and ran quickly to tell Mammy what the driver had said. Pockets knew it must be important because Mammy hurriedly went into the house to tell Ms. Martha.

Ms. Martha went to the front door and as she was going out onto the porch she could see the driver and he was helping a white lady out of the carriage.

Ms. Martha invited her to come and sit on the porch with her. The lady was very poised with dignity and manner.

The driver then left them to their talk and he went to the back of the house where he knew he could find some one to talk with.

The weather was still plenty warm and Mammy brought a big container of cool lemonade for them to drink while they were talking.

The lady told Ms. Martha that she had talked to Dr. Wise in town and he recommended that she come here because Ms. Martha would most likely help her. She stated that her situation needed to be kept a secret as much as possible. She stated that she was going to have a baby, and by all indications it would be a negro baby.

Ms. Martha knew and could tell by now that the lady was pregnant but this statement was a surprise to her.

The lady would not say where she was from or

would she say what her name was, she did state that Washington, Georgia was quite a distance from where she lived.

She needed to have someone she could trust and depend on and Dr. Wise told her that Ms. Martha was the one she could count on and he was sure she would give her the help she needed.

The lady told Ms. Martha that she would be more than willing to pay for any trouble she might cause and would gladly pay for her stay. She knew Ms. Martha had plenty of help and there were young girls around with babies and she stated she intended to give her the baby when it was born as she never wanted to see it.

Ms. Martha knew the lady was from a prominent family from her manner, clothes and jewelry.

The driver had gone to the back of the big house and was looking around. Mammy came out and says, "What are you doing here and what is your name?" He replied, Jim. Mammy says they ain't no one with just one name. She says are you a "Smart-aleck, high stepping, nigger, with gold teeth?" She said that if the Lord had of wanted you to have gold teeth he would have given them to you.

The negro driver was tall, real black and shiny. A gold watch chain was hanging from his pocket, and flashy rings on his fingers.

Mammy said to him, I saw you looking at my girls and they all belong to me. You mess around here and if you break one of my girls hearts, you better hope that I don't mistake your mouth for a gold mine and decide to collect me some gold.

For all I know you may not be any better than poor white trash. All of these darkies are mine, and I love dem all. We are quality folks and we don't need no little pick-a-ninnies dat ain't got no daddy. I'll knock you from amazing grace to a floating opportunity, now git.

This was Mammy's way of setting him straight. Jim could see he wasn't too welcome so he went back to the front of the big house where the carriage was.

Pockets and Stovepipe was examining the carriage with all it's polished brass. Jim was standing by looking proud.

Pockets says to Stovepipe, "Could this wagon go a hundred miles in a day." Stovepipe says yes, it could go further than dat. Pockets says could it go a thousand miles in one day. Stovepipe says, "If it got started real early in the morning it could."

Pockets agreeing and says if I was not so black I would ride in dis wagon. Stovepipe says I don't care how black I is, I would ride in it anyway.

Willie was looking all over for them and he says if you all don't git away from that carriage and do yo chores, Mammy will make you think dat you is riding in it.

Ms. Martha and the lady had been talking for some time, and Ms. Martha consented that she could stay as long as necessary.

The driver brought the ladies belongings in

the big house and took them to her room. He then returned to the carriage and drove off.

Ms. Martha and the lady had many long conversations as they sat on the front porch. Ms. Martha thought she should have a name other than the "white lady." Ms. Martha decided to just call her "Missy," that was fine with the lady.

Through the conversations she talked a lot about Mississippi, especially Jackson.

Missy had been there over a month and her time was getting closer.

Mrs. Briarfield was watching everything that was going on. She was thinking the white lady could be the answer to her dream. She looked at her as being able to have their own plantation. She wanted her daughters in society.

She had a plan in mind, so she told her husband about the plan. She told him that when Missy has her baby and starts home, that he should follow her and find where she came from.

She could see by the diamonds she wore and her expensive clothes that she must have money.

Mr. Briarfield was a little reluctant to go for this at first but she knew with a little pressure he could be persuaded to go along with the idea.

Mrs. Briarfield knew how important Ms. Martha and Missy wanted the secret kept, but she wanted something more for herself and her daughters.

There was never a secret that was able to be kept on a plantation. In no time at all it was all over about the white lady that had come to have her baby.

Ms. Martha and Missy would sit on the big front porch and talk for hours. She told Missy about her trip when she was a child, when her mother and daddy moved from Charleston to Washington.

How they had helped a run-a-way slave escape from the patroler. How he came to live with them. He helped build their house and his cabin. He and her daddy cleared land for the so called King Cotton.

Mo then went to work on the plantation so they could have extra money.

She told Missy about Mo saving her life from the mad dog, while saving her he had been bitten and died.

How Tom Boggs tried to warn us that the dog was coming, Mo put me on a limb, as he saw I had frozen in the trail and could not move. As he was standing under the tree holding me, the dog bit him. He died in about two weeks and a half. I blame myself for freezing in the trail as I could have stepped aside, the dog would have gone on by and Mo would still be alive. While he was dying he asked my daddy to go ahead and kill him. Daddy said he could not do that, but if it were possible he would trade places with him.

Mo would tell me animal stories that he remembered when he was a child and would make me dolls out of sticks. I really do miss him.

Missy said, "I have heard said that cream will rise to the top whether in a cabin or in a mansion." Seems to me that was Mo's finest hour.

This big sacrifice that Mo had made for Martha had bothered her ever since.

She told Missy how her daddy had been killed by the Indian, and how Massa William bought their farm and they moved to the plantation.

This is how she and Massa William came to know each other and got married. But in a few years he was dead, leaving me four months pregnant.

This is how I became owner of the Peteet plantation. It was a big responsibility because I was very young at the time.

CHAPTER 15

Ms. Martha's only son, Rabun Hood was now a year old.

Dr. Wise checked on Missy regularly. Her driver came by everyday but did not stay.

A few days later Missy and Ms. Martha were sitting on the front porch and Missy started having labor pains. Immediately they sent for Dr. Wise.

Three days she was in hard labor. Dr. Wise told Martha she was having a hard time because of the circumstances, on the third day she gave birth to a fine big boy. He was of medium color.

Missy did not want to see the baby, so it was taken away by Mammy. The baby was put with a young girl that had just had a baby of her own. She was able to nurse both of them. Of course Mammy was in charge as always.

When Mammy saw the baby she groaned and said, "Another pick-a-ninnie" just what we need and she grumbled "work, work, work."

In about two weeks Missy was ready to leave as she had fully recovered. The driver came and was ready to take her home.

As she was leaving Ms. Martha asked her what name shall we give the boy? Missy said she did not care. Missy had talked a lot about Jackson, Mississippi, so Ms. Martha said why don't we call him Jackson, this seemed to please Missy a lot.

As she was leaving, she turned to Ms. Martha and handed her a large envelope, she said this will take care of all the expenses. When Ms. Martha looked to see what was in the envelope, she saw there was a large sum of money in large bills. She was reluctant to take the money at first but then she thought Jackson would probably need it in later years.

She took the money and put it in a vault that had been built in the rocks in the fire place. She never used it.

CHAPTER 16

Jim Briarfield watched as Missy's carriage pulled out of sight and rounded the corner from the plantation.

Jim mounted his horse and started following a short distance behind. Soon they were both out of sight.

Mrs. Briarfield went to Ms. Martha and told her that Jim had to leave unexpectedly and would be returning soon.

Before Jim left he had put one of his field hands in charge. Jock, a 60 year old that he trusted and had been on the plantation all his life. He was to be in charge of things until Jim returned.

Ms. Martha was not happy about this and thought it kinda strange that someone had alredy been put in charge.

She still was not happy about this but guessed it would work out as the crops had already been planted and Jim did make a good overseer. He knew all about the plantation because his daddy had been overseer for several years before he died. Jim had taken his place.

In just a short time all the field hands were being disrupted and they thought that Jock, the newly appointed overseer was showing favoritism among them.

As time went on things settled down and was working a little smoother. The crops were doing fine and it looked as if it would be a bumper crop. It hadn't been too good the year before and was hoping this year would be a good one.

Days passed and Ms. Martha asked Mrs. Briarfield if she had any word from Jim. She said no, and that she should not worry because he would be home soon.

In the meantime Mrs. Briarfield had been strutting around for days making remarks to the negros that they would probably not be around much longer and would be needing some help for their own plantation when Jim returned.

A couple of weeks had passed and still no word from Jim. Mrs. Briarfield was looking worried and was very quiet.

Another week passed, she couldn't keep quiet any longer. She broke down and went to Ms. Martha telling her everything about the plot and what they had planned to do.

Jim believed that Missy must be wealthy but not knowing her name or where she was from, Jim would have to follow her. He hoped she would pay him for keeping quiet about her baby. Then with all the money they could buy their own plantation, their two girls could be in society and marry rich and could join social clubs.

By confessing this to Ms. Martha she was hoping they would help find Jim.

Ms. Martha decided that if Jim did return, she could not trust him again. She told Mrs. Briarfield that she would have to move. After much begging and pleading Ms. Martha changed her mind because Mrs. Briarfield had no place to go, she let her stay on certain conditions.

Each evening when Mrs. Briarfield was finished with her chores, she would go out to the road that passed by the plantation and sit for long periods at a time, hoping that Jim might be coming home. This went on for several months, and she finally realized that Jim was not coming back. Jim was never seen or heard of again.

It is believed that while Jim was following Missy's carriage that he was killed by one of her guards. They knew she had more protection than just the driver of her carriage. She had traveled from Mississippi, which was through two states. She had to have plenty of protection. It was too dangerous for a lady to travel alone.

Others believe Jim could have been killed by Indians, just for his horse or anything they could get.

Mammy hearing about Jim, says they are just trying to be what they already is, "poor white trash."

The Briarfield girls were helping in the big house, Mammy was teaching them to cook and clean. Their names were Mandy and Matilda. Mrs. Briarfield was also helping with all the chores.

No one worked on Saturday or Sunday, only what had to be done.

Each Sunday Ms. Martha hired a preacher to come to the plantation and hold services for them. Anyone that felt the need to attend the services could do so.

The preacher arrived early at the big house and was getting acquainted with everyone. He was about 35 years of age, tall, with curly hair and fair skin.

Mrs. Briarfield seemed to like him right away and they talked a lot. After the services was over, he spent the day there and it was getting late. Mrs. Briarfield insisted he stay the night and get an early start in the morning back to Savannah. The preacher thought this was a good idea, so he graciously accepted the invitation.

After all her husband had been gone for ten years and she was probably in need of some spiritual condolence.

After staying the night in the Briarfield house, he informed Ms. Martha that he needed to stay the week and would be there for the next Sunday's service and he would preach then for free. If he was able to spend the week there he could probably save some souls and keep them from going to hell.

A few weeks later, in the middle of the night, Mrs. Briarfield went running to the big house and said she had just been raped. The next morning they sent for the sheriff.

Mrs. Briarfield told the sheriff she had been out walking because she was unable to sleep. Someone came up behind her, threw something over her head and raped her. She couldn't see who it was.

It was hard for the sheriff to believe this, as Mrs. Briarfiel kept changing her story, it was different each time she would tell it.

As Mrs. Briarfield was talking, Mammy was getting madder by the minute, because this was making her so called children look bad and she was not going to stand for it.

After Mrs. Briarfield had finished talking with the sheriff, Mammy called her outside. She told her she better tell Ms. Martha the truth about the whole thing or she was going to.

Mammy told Mrs. Briarfield how she had seen her and that so called "Bible Thumping Preacher" together. She said when I came after you to work, I was standing on your porch, the shade was up and I could see everything. So you better tell Ms. Martha what went on or I'm going to. You're just lucky that I'm giving you dis chance to talk before I do. This looks bad on all us quality folks and everyone else too.

Mrs. Briarfield went to Ms. Martha and told her the whole story.

How she told the preacher that Jim had been gone a long time and she missed him. How they had wanted a plantation and her girls could be in society and wear pretty clothes. He told me that I was what he had been looking for and that he had a big mansion in Savannah. He would come back for me and we would get married. Her girls would be able to meet a lot of eligible bachelors.

He said he could not wait to have me and I believed him. Missing my period, I thought I might be pregnant. I know now I am not. I was scared and decided to say I was raped, I know how foolish I was.

Ms. Martha told her, "I don't think you could

do anything else that would surprise me anymore." I should have checked that so called preacher out better anyway, because he made me look foolish too. He heard I needed a preacher and thinking it was a good chance to make some quick money, he borrowed a Bible and called himself a preacher and I believed him.

Mammy would call that "double white trash."

The sheriff may want to talk to you later about a false claim. Maybe he won't be too hard on you.

CHAPTER 17

It was getting late at the big house and everyone was ready for bed. Mammy tells Ms. Martha they is looking for someone over at Massa Hanks place. They is going through the fields with lighted torches.

Ms. Martha says Hank has a lot of trouble at his place, his slaves are always running away. Mammy says what makes him so mean? Ms. Martha says he cannot get along with anyone, probably because of the way he was brought up.

Just then, there was scratching and then a knock on the back door. Mammy goes to the door and says, "Lordy Be," if it ain't Ola May. Her clothes were ripped and she looked a mess. Mammy said, "Child git yo-sef in here, is dey looking fo you? Did yo run-a-way?"

Ola May was 16 years old, Hank had said she was retarded but could do some simple chores. When she didn't do what Hank wanted, or forgot what he told her to do, he was angry with her. Sometimes denying her food, saying "No work, no eat."

Ms. Martha had been sorry for Ola May for sometime, she didn't realize how that poor girl had suffered until she and Mammy examined her frail body. She looked like she never had a full meal and was wearing rags for clothes. She was very nervous and afraid.

Ms. Martha and Mammy were expecting to see Hank anytime now, they were not disappointed.

Hank knocking and calling to Ms. Martha to open

up, saying I got to talk to you. Ms. Martha told Mammy to hide Ola May, she then went to the door. He says where is that little run-a-way negro, I know she is here and I'm going to search the house until I find her, you know there is a law about helping run-a-way slaves escape. Are you hiding her?

Ms. Martha says yes, she is in the house but you are not going to get her tonight. Tomorrow you get the sheriff and a search warrant, that's the only way you are going to search my house.

Hank said by the time I do that you will hide her some place, what do you want to do, make her like your fat negros and giving them two days a week off. Martha you set a bad example for the others, soon they will all want the same. You have ruined your negros.

We all got to work if we eat, your negros are lazy as sin and won't work.

Ms. Martha told him they made a lot more cotton than he did and I don't have any run-a-way to look for either. Hank said last year he got some bad seed is what happened. Besides no one gave me a plantation, I worked for what I got. We are not all rich like you, but some day I'm going to be richer than you, you wait and see.

Now you bring Ola May out or I'll find her myself. Ms. Martha says I am not going to bring her out to you and you are not going to look for her in this house, you are so ignorant I don't know why I even talk to you, but I'll do this, I will buy her from you. Better think on that because you are not getting her back tonight. I never saw you when you would turn down money.

Ole Hank blew his cool, says he won't sell and he's going to search the house and find her, he was cussing and threatening of course.

Mammy was listening outside the room but came busting in, with her shotgun leveled at Hanks head. She says I don't mess with white folks business but this shotgun talks to me and it says, "Massa Hank yo better git or yo will be going back carrying your head under yo arm."

Hank, was plenty scared lookin down that gun barrel with Mammy's finger on the trigger. It was not what he was countin on, in fact he was plain scared and was taken back a notch.

He said to Mammy, (she still had the gun pointed at his head), you talk to a gun and the gun talks back. Woman you are a witch, she says I guess so. I have a broom too, and some moon lit night I may come visit you on my broom. But in the day time I'm jist a 300 pound black mammy looking after all my children on the plantation. Hank saw he was beaten, saying he would be back with the sheriff in the morning.

After Hank left, Ms. Martha says "Mammy put that gun up before it goes off." Mammy says it was not loaded anyway and they had a good laugh. Ms. Martha says Mammy I don't know how anyone could do without you.

Mammy says we have got to do something for Ole May. Ms. Martha says tomorrow is another day and

I'll bet we can handle Hank. Let's get some rest now because it is late.

The next morning Hank and the sheriff shows up. The sheriff asked Ms. Martha if Ola May was there, she said yes. He asked her why she was keeping Hanks girl, she said come with me and I'll show you why.

Looking at the poor girl, starved, half naked, she says if she goes back to him, in time he will starve her to death. I offered to buy her from him but he refuses to sell her. I am swearing out a complaint for extreme cruelty to a slave and I expect you to arrest him, I'll drag him through all the courts if necessary. The sheriff knew she meant what she said.

He told her he would talk to Hank, they talked for a long time and Hank decided to sell Ola May to Ms. Martha. She paid him twice as much as he could get on the market for her but she and Mammy got Ola May. Hank says she was not much anyway. He told Ms. Martha to keep that witch off his property.

Mammy puts her arm around Ola May and says we love you, and ain't no one goin to hurt you no more. I'm going to make you pretty with new clothes and you'll have lots to eat. Ola May says I love you and I want to stay here forever and ever.

Now Stovepipe and Pockets were working in the barn. Pockets says to Stovepipe, "Could you put a million dollars in your pocket?" Stovepipe says, "No, it would take two pockets." Pockets says you sure are smart. I wish I had a million dollars in my pockets right now. Stovepipe says if you had a million dollars would you give me half of it? Pockets says I would not give you a penny of it or I would not loan you any of it, you probably would not pay me back anyway. Pockets says you have as much right to wish for a million dollars as I do. Sho we is friends, we work together cleaning the barn and feeding chickens and stock and looking after the yard, but I'm goin buy me a riding horse with my million dollars and dats dat.

Willie, hearing the talking, says if Mammy comes down here and sees the mess in this barn you'll both be her riding horse.

Willie had just about all he could take, trying to get work out of those two. For sometime he had been asking Mammy to let him go back to the fields where his friends were. He was about to go crazy riding herd on Stovepipe and Pockets, they had to be watched in everything they did.

Mammy had Ola May looking pretty. In about two days she decided to let Willie put Ola May in charge of Stovepipe and Pockets and he could return to the fields. She knew Ola May could do the job because there was nothing wrong with her except she was just afraid of Ole Hank.

Willie went back to the fields and Ola May did her job.

Mammy says she should have shot Ole Hank when she had the chance.

CHAPTER 18

It was the year of 1860. Rabun and Jackson were sixteen years of age. They lived in the big house and were treated as brothers.

Rabun was a very easy going person but Jackson had a quick temper. It was hard for him to come to terms with himself as to who he really was.

While Jackson was in the big house he was treated just like anyone else that lived there, but when he was outside on the grounds and around the fields, the negros did not accept him because he acted like a biggety negro. He acted as though he was better than they were. This didn't help the situation any because Jackson knew they didn't like him anyway.

Rabun and Jackson had been tutored since they were five years old. They were both quick learners. They had also been given music lessons. Rabun played the violin and Jackson the banjo. Professor Bone came to the big house and gave them lessons.

Professor Bone was a Cajan from Louisiana. The boys were easy to learn and in no time at all they were playing Cajan music. Professor Bone said he had never seen such talent in all his days, he was very proud of them.

They were playing so well that they were in demand to play for square dances. Sometimes they played all night. Their tone, the beat and the rhythm was all Cajan.

One time they were asked to play at the Boggs house. When the music started, Ole Tom Boggs started patting his foot on the floor, he took a big swig out of his jug and before long he was ready to dance. No one had ever seen such dancing out of Ole Tom. First he did the pigeon wing, then the Turkey Trot, and then the Buzzard Bounce. No one could believe he had it in him.

Tom stops dancing and takes another big swig from his jug. He says his boys make the best corn whiskey there is and it is in demand because it is the best. He samples every batch that is made. Tom says there is good whiskey, then there is middle whiskey, then there is rot-gut whiskey. The one's that make the rot-gut ought be made to drink it all. Tom says good whiskey goes down smooth and has a kick like a Georgia mule, and the next morning you wake up feeling good.

Dr. Wise ask Tom how much whiskey did he drank, Tom says how much whiskey is there? Dr. Wise says I don't know how much whiskey there is, and Tom says if you don't know how much whiskey there is how do you expect me to know how much I drink.

Dr. Wise told Tom he was a living double miracle. First, that he had any liver left at all from drinking so much and second, how he raised two boys to be good solid boys that they were. Tom says it was not easy but I just stayed with it, that's how.

Rabun and Jackson were in such demand to play for dances and had so many invitations they could not keep up with them all. They had become local celebrities with their violin and banjo playing.

Ms. Martha was visited often by her Uncle Glover

Crain. He lived in Charleston and was a speck-a-lator in cotton and slaves.

Ms. Martha's overseer, Jock, was getting old and the job of looking after everything was getting too much for him to handle. After all he had been there since Briarfield had left. He needed something easier to do.

Ms. Martha asked Uncle Glover to bring her someone that could take over as overseer. In less than a month he brought her a negro about sixty years of age. He was from the west Indies, his name was Tu Saint. He was tall, educated talking and well read. He was also a professed preacher. With him came a girl of mixed race. Everyone presumed this girl was his daughter, her name was La Rose.

La Rose was a pretty girl, about fifteen years old with very light skin. Ms. Martha was happy to get them both. La Rose helped in the big house and Tu Saint went with Jock to the fields.

In a few weeks Tu Saint was able to take full charge of everything. Jock was able to do what ever was easy for him, but most of the time he was just sitting under the shade of a tree, he had earned a long rest.

La Rose was a girl that any boy would stop and take a second look at. Rabun was no exception. But of course there was always Mammy watching what was going on. She had made a believer out of those two boys long ago.

CHAPTER 19

The talk through the plantations was always about war. The war had not started yet, some believed it would never come, but others said if it did happen it would be over in a month, because no one would dare make war on king cotton.

The cotton was needed in the north for their mills and it was believed England could not do without cotton. The South never believed that England could not get cotton from anywhere but from them.

The South also would not believe that anyone could whip the South in battle. The Southern boys believed that one good southern could whip any ten, chicken stealing yanks. Most of the young boys were worried that if the war did start, it would be over before they could get joined up.

General Sherman told General Lee that it would be useless for him to think he could whip the North, because they had all the factories. The South didn't worry, because they thought that England would help them if they went to war because of their need for the king cotton. England did not readily offer help to anyone.

Uncle Glover visited Ms. Martha often. On one of his visits he told her that she should start getting rid of her negros or at least free them. He told her that it was almost certain there was going to be a war and they would be freed anyway. Ms. Martha said she would give it some thought. Her conclusion was, the plantation owners and the negros both alike live off the plantation for all their needs. They are tied together, one to the other.

How would the negros survive if they were freed. How would the old that can't work, the sick that can't help themselves, and the young, how would they all survive. No one is big enough to handle this except maybe the government. If all the slaves are freed it will be the governments responsibility to care for them.

There were only a few who believed there would even be a war. Cotton had brought all the good things to the South and Old King Cotton would take care of them now.

It was now 1860 and in a few months the North and South would be fighting in one of the bloodiest of wars.

The plantation was having one of its biggest bumper crop of cotton they had ever had. Tu Saint was the best overseer Ms. Martha had ever had. This was their best year yet. Tu Saint had a pleasing way about him, but he was also very firm with the field hands.

Mammy and Tu Saint were getting along very nicely, she liked preachers and he preached every Sunday at the plantation. He was smart enough to keep the sermons short and to the point.

When Tu Saint first started holding the sermons, there were very few that attended, but when Mammy made it known that everyone who attends to hear Tu Saint preach will get a big meal. After that announcement there was a considerable larger crowd in the services.

Mammy loved quality folks and Tu Saint was truly that.

Rabun had been trying to get La Rose's attention for sometime, but she just acted as though he was not there. She liked him very much but she didn't want him to think she was too anxious.

In the big house La Rose's room was on the same floor as was Rabun's and Jackson's.

Mammy and Ms. Martha stayed on the first floor, along with Tu Saint.

With Rabun and LaRose in the upstairs rooms, this made it easier for Rabun to give La Rose more attention without Mammy knowing everything that went on.

CHAPTER 20

After the war began in 1861, everyone thought it would be over soon. But little did they know the South's golden years were coming to an end and bad times were on the way.

It's like Shakespeare says, "Life is a stage with many characters, each playing a different part." First, there was Mammy urging her people to be quality folks. Then there was Ola May, she was riding watch on Stovepipe and Pockets, she would not let them get away with anything. Willie had gone back to the field where his friends were.

There was the Boggs family, Tom drank his whiskey, but never made a drop. Jeff and Frank made whiskey but never drank any of it. They quit farming because whiskey making was much more lucrative. Those two boys had their heads on straight because when the sheriff wanted Jeff to attend a dinner in his honor for killing the Indian, Jeff said that it just had to be and I am not going to celebrate killing anyone.

Then there is Mrs. Briarfield. The reason they called her Mrs. Briarfield was she didn't like her maiden name and she never told anyone what it was. She goes from cabin to cabin spreading gossip. The field hands named her "Bring a bone, take a bone, Briarfield."

Ole Professor Bone went back to Louisiana with the sheriff, seems he had married too many women and never got a divorce.

Rabun and Jackson, with a lot of talent and work from professor Bone, they were now local celebrities. Rabun with eyes for La Rose and Jackson still didn't know what he wanted.

Then the two Briarfield girls were still looking for husbands. Mammy says they first got to have a boy friend and they ain't never did that yet.

Ms. Martha had never told Jackson about the money that was left by his mother. She did plan on giving it to him someday, but was wondering if it would be a blessing or a curse. She hadn't needed it and was saving it for him. Ms. Martha looked at both the boys as her own anyway.

As the war progressed, Rabun was drafted in the State as a home guard. This was all he could do as he had a bad knee from an accident when he was a small boy. He patroled the area around Washington, looking for Yankee spies.

The war was going good for the South for awhile, but supplies were getting very short. The North had blockaded the sea coast and it was stopping any supplies from coming in.

There was very little salt left and it was very much in demand. Such a demand that the farmers were digging in their smoke houses in hopes of finding a little salt that could be used to preserve their meat.

Coffee was also at a premium, no one had any at all. Everything was in short supply.

Ms. Martha was still able to produce plenty of cotton on her plantation, but there was no way to sell the cotton. The blockage had stopped everything from going out or anything from coming in. But the worse was yet to come.

Rabun stayed home most of the time. He and La Rose had become very close, she loved him and thought that he loved her. He would come into her room at night and stay until morning, this was a common practice for about a year.

They were not fooling Mammy or Ms. Martha about what was going on and everything was going smooth until one day she informed him that she was pregnant, she asked him what he was going to do about it? He was worried greatly about it and told her he would think of something. He would do anything to keep this from his mother. La Rose would have liked to have married Rabun but this was not permissible.

Rabun told La Rose they could put the blame on Jackson, but La Rose got real upset and said she would not do such a thing to Jackson. She told him it was his baby and she would not lie about it.

La Rose went to Ms. Martha and Mammy and told them the whole story. It was not too much of a surprise to them.

Rabun knew if he stayed around that his mother would be upset over the ordeal, so he left for awhile until things settled down again.

In a few months Dr. Wise delivered La Rose's baby, a beautiful, healthy boy.

Rabun always rode a fine, fiery horse. One day he saw La Rose at the wash house and he rode down to ask about the baby. He got off the horse and tied him to a tree near by, the baby was lying on a blanket under the tree.

As he and La Rose were talking, they got into an argument, which they did almost every time they came in contact with each other. La Rose was mad and she threw a wet rag at Rabun, instead of hitting him, it hit the horse. This causing the horse to spook and as he rared up, he stepped on the baby, killing him instantly.

Dr. Wise came and he said there was nothing

he or anyone could do for the baby. The horse had stepped on the baby's chest, crushing him.

CHAPTER 21

La Rose and Rabun were very upset over the tragic death of their child, and were blaming each other for what happened.

La Rose was hurt because of the way Rabun had been responding toward her, she thought that he had really loved her for herself and not just for her body. She would not talk to him and wanted to hurt him. She hoped she would never see him again, and she vowed she would never give herself to another man without real love.

The war between the North and South was getting worse. Rabun and Jackson was still in demand to play for dances. Jackson was not only playing his banjo but he was now singing as they played.

They were desired by the girls wherever they went because they both were very handsome boys.

Jackson had not been too interested in the opposite sex up until now, but things were beginning to change. He was what you might call a late bloomer.

The girls were attracted to Jackson but seems the only one he could think about was La Rose. She was more desirable to him than anyone else.

La Rose would have nothing to do with Jackson, she had all she wanted of him and Rabun. This was painful to Jackson's ego, as he had seen her around with Willie, the field hand.

Jackson thought, what could a field hand offer her that he could not give her. Jackson tried to show her how he felt but she would have nothing to do with him.

La Rose went to Mammy and told her what was going on. She told Mammy she wanted Jackson to leave her and Willie alone. Mammy takes Jackson aside and says to him, I took care of you from the first day you was born. Fed, bathed, and diapered you, you are just another one of my children on the plantation, doing your thing, that's all you is. Dat girl don't want nothin to do with you and I don't care if you do like her, anyway what's so bad about being a field hand. Willie is a good boy and got his head on straight too.

Mammy asked Jackson, can you eat the music you make? No, but you eat the food Willie grows. Which is more important? Food or music, you ain't no better or no worse than a field hand. Remember we are quality folks, thats what we is and you let Willie and La Rose be. Everyone has to find their own place and if you can't you will go from amazing grace to a floatin opportunity and thats worse than nothing.

Mammy's advice lasted for only a short while, for Jackson could not forget La Rose. She and Willie were still seeing each other and he couldn't stand it any longer.

One day Jackson got Willie behind the cabin and they had a big fight. Jackson beat Willie up real bad. La Rose knew she had to do something, so she went to talk to Tu Saint, asking him to keep Jackson away from them.

Tu Saint told Ms. Martha what was going on, and he told her that if Jackson was seen hanging around the cabin again that Willie's friends, which he had many, would probably kill Jackson because they did not like what he was doing to Willie.

Ms. Martha was very sad over this and she told Tu Saint she knew Rabun and Jackson were spoiled and had been for years. Everyone in the big house was guilty of this except Mammy and guess I have been the worse of all.

Ms. Martha told Tu Saint that Willie was in charge and he had to talk to Jackson in no uncertain terms. We can't have this going on and I want to know what happens.

A couple of days later Tu Saint found Jackson in the barn, he was rubbing his horse down. Tu Saint starts talking to Jackson about the weather but soon the conversation turned to Willie and La Rosa.

Jackson went from denial to anger. Calling Tu saint a boot licking nigger preacher and that he would fix him like he did Willie. He told Tu Saint if he wasn't so old he would work him over worse than he did Willie. Jackson was so angry that he let Tu Saint have a jab in the mouth and one on the nose. Tu Saint hit Jackson on the chin, knocking him down.

Jackson got up, pulls out his knife which he always carried and took a swipe at Tu Saint, cutting him across the chest. Tu Saint grabs a single-tree that was hanging on the wall and let Jackson have it across the head, splitting his skull. In a few minutes Jackson was dead.

Jackson's death was a great tragedy for Ms. Martha and she went into shock.

Mammy says Jackson just couldn't take it, he could not understand why anyone would turn him down for a field hand, because he was so popular.

La Rose liked Willie, he was kind to her and no doubt he loved her, but she was only using him to get back at Rabun, deep down she still loved Rabun, but wished she didn't.

Ms. Martha offered Tu Saint and La Rose their freedom because of what had happened. She thought maybe they couldn't cope with it.

Tu Saint told Ms. Martha that he had already had his freedom once, and he had rather be a overseer slave on a good plantation than be a freed homeless ex-slave.

La Rose took her freedom and the money Ms. Martha gave her. She went up north somewhere to live.

Rabun missed Jackson more than any of the rest. He still played his music for awhile but it just wasn't the same, he just lost interest.

The following Sunday Tu Saint prayed for Jackson and asked for forgiveness for killing him.

CHAPTER 22

The South was gaining in the war on one day and losing on the next.

Ms. Martha was one of the many plantation owners that had generously supported the South. She bought thousands of dollars of war bonds, but this was not enough, they needed so very much more of everything.

Most of the negro slaves were wanting their freedom but they really didn't know what they were asking for. They were soon to find out. If you were hungry and no place to go, freedom was not free.

Rabun still patroled the area looking for Yankee deserters.

Mammy and Ring were out in the yard one morning and thought they got the smell of coffee being brewed. This had happened before and the aroma was coming from the Briarfield house, so they decided to investigate. Even when you had been without coffee for such a long time you could still remember the aroma.

The South had no coffee, as all supplies were blocked from coming in and hadn't had any coffee for several years.

Mammy and Ring went to the Briarfield house and looked in the window. There they saw a Yankee soldier sitting at the table sipping coffee, big as life. Both the Briarfield girls were there and waiting on him, hand and foot.

Mammy hurried back to the big house and told Rabun what she had seen. He was preparing to leave on his patrol so he immediately went to the Briarfield house.

Rabun tries the door, but it was locked. When Mrs. Briarfield saw that it was Rabun, she opened the door. Rabun asked, "Where is the Yankee soldier that was here?" But before Mrs. Briarfield could answer, Rabun saw a foot sticking out from under the bed. He drew his pistol and told the soldier to come out or he would shoot. The soldier quickly came crawling from under the bed, dragging his leg.

The reason for the lame leg was, sometime back the soldier had been wounded in the leg and had tried to hide under some bushes until he healed. The Briarfield girls were out walking and found him hiding, they took him back to their house and cared for him until he was better. Rabun knew then why he hadn't seen him, because the girls had him in the house. The soldier had the coffee in his pack.

The girls had been looking after him real good, in fact the oldest girl was already pregnant.

Rabun took the soldier to Washington and he was turned over to the Confederate army.

Mammy says anyone can get a boyfriend if you look hard enough and if you don't care what you get.

1864. The war had taken a turn for the worse for the South. General Sherman had advanced down as far as Atlanta and had burned the town.

Sherman and his troops were marching to Savannah. His army made a sixty mile wide sweep through the state.

To keep them going, they lived off the land

as they went through taking anything of value and whatever they needed.

They burned the houses and barns, they raped and stole and killed.

The fall of Atlanta was the breaking point for the south, but the war still went on for sometime before it was officially ended.

Ms. Martha was informed that a company of Yankee's were headed to her plantation. She knew if they found her silver and jewelry that they would take it, so she quickly put it in a basket and dropped it down the well, hoping that would save it.

A short time later, the troops arrived at the big house. There were approximately two hundred calvary soldiers. The Captain dismounted and Ms. Martha met him on the front lawn. She told him he could take whatever he needed but please do not burn the house and barn. That would be of no military value to him.

The Captain was young and very polite. He asked Ms. Martha if she had any confederate troops in the house or on the property? She stated there is no one here but the slaves and no one will give you any trouble but you are welcome to look.

The Captain told Ms. Martha they would camp there for the night and would be leaving in the morning. We will not search your house and will not harm you. We are living off the land and because of that we will take what ever we need, such as food, stock, wagons and anything else we can use.

By this time the negros had surrounded the toops,

the soldiers had invited the negros to go along with them and get their freedom. The Yankee troops made it sound so good, like they would not only have their freedom but it would also be like a Beulah land.

The slaves believed Beulah land was a Heaven right here on earth, with no more work, no pain, and no sorrow.

When morning came and with the help of the slaves the troops stripped the plantation of all the chickens, hogs, cows, horses and wagons they could find. When there was nothing else of value, they left.

Almost all the negro slaves were following behind the troops, even the sick and crippled were riding in the wagons.

Of course Stovepipe and Pockets were with them and they could hardly wait until they got to Beulah land. They each had a ham under their arm.

Pockets said to Stovepipe, when we get to Beulah land are we going to have to clean the barn? Stovepipe says the barns don't need cleaning in Beulah land, they clean themselves.

Pockets says Ola May ain't smart enough to get within a mile of Beulah land, they don't take dumb people and besides she stayed at the big house with Mammy.

She's always saying, do this, do that, or I'll tell Mammy, I hope I never see her again.

No, I didn't say it was a mile to Beulah land, it's more like ten miles, Pockets you are so dumb, and you can't hear either.

Pockets said is Beulah land bigger than Ms. Martha's plantation? Stovepipe says twice as big. Sure hope it don't get full before we get there. The Yankee soldiers said there was plenty of room. I'd hate to go back and work for Ola May.

CHAPTER 23

Mammy was disgusted with her quality folks, but they were still her children.

She told Ms. Martha that she would like to get her hands on every one of dem, dey is worse dan poor white trash. When dey were here, dat is as close as any of dem will ever git to Beulah land. Dem Yankee's jest made a fool of dem, next dey will be trying to find the end of the rainbow.

Ms. Martha asked Mammy, if you truly believed there was a place like Beulah land, wouldn't you go with them? Mammy said she had all the Beulah land right here that she wanted.

All that was left now on the plantation was Ms. Martha, Ring, Mrs. Briarfield, her two daughters, Mammy, Ola Mae, and Rabun.

Ms. Martha never forgot how Ring loved Mo and how Mo had saved her life, at the cost of his. She thought about Mo often and hoped she was worthy of Mo giving his life for her.

Ms. Martha told Mammy that she had given two fortunes to helping the war, but its what I believed in and now everything is gone. If all the negros were to come back, I wouldn't have any stock, wagons, or horses. No money to buy any supplies. Maybe its just as well they left and I hope they find a good place.

To be honest, I don't know what we are going to do. The taxes on this place have been raised three times this year. I've been notified to pay them or the property is going up for sale. They call that business, but this kind of business is what broke the South.

In a few weeks the negro slaves started coming back, begging to be taken in. Ms. Martha expected them all to return before long. Some of the ones that were sick and the old died before they could get back.

The negros soon found that their freedom left them homeless, hungry and ragged. Beulah land had evaded them. They also found the freedom they experienced was not worth much. They stole till there was nothing left to steal.

Its like Ms. Martha said, if they had stayed and not left, what could they have done here. The Yankee's had taken all their stock, wagons and food.

As expected, Stovepipe and Pockets were among the first to return. Ola May got her job back of looking after them, they were even glad to see her.

In a few weeks there were about fifty more returned and wanted to be taken back.

Ms. Martha's plantation was broke, but in another way she was not. She still had the money that Jackson's mother had given her to raise him, she had put the money in safe keeping and never used any of it and had never counted it.

She was going to give it to Jackson when he needed it. She felt Jackson would have wanted her to use the money if she needed it.

She took the money from where it had been hidden so long and counted it. Much to her surprise it turned out to be a hundred thousand dollars in good currency.

Ms. Martha knew she had to put the money to good use, so the first thing she did was pay the taxes so the plantation would be safe again. Then she bought all the things that had been taken from the plantation. The plantation was ready for operation again.

Money was very scarce and a dollar was worth a lot more than just face value.

Ms. Martha aloted each one a plot of ground to work as their own. They were given what was needed for them to get started and after that they furnished their own supplies. They had a house to live in, food to eat and a plot of ground like their own so they were happy again.

These freed negros were now what was known as sharecroppers. They got a part of the crop and the owner got a part.

Mammy says she is glad that some of them came back but she wanted to put them straight. First of all, if there was a place like Beulah land, which da ain't, you all couldn't git in unless dey had cotton for you to pick. Your Beulah land is when your fields are full of white cotton, food on the table and someone dat loves you. Money in your pockets and goin to town every Saturday to spend it and preaching on Sunday.

Dat is Beulah land.

CHAPTER 24

A year or so had passed and it was now 1867. The war was over.

Hank, the farmer that had lived on land adjoining the Peteet plantation was now broke.

He was blaming everyone but himself for his loss and mostly the Peteet's. Swearing he would get even with them for everything that had happened to him.

His farm had been taken for back taxes and unpaid debts.

With nothing to do now, he spent most of his time in town, drinking and talking to anyone that would listen to him.

Rabun was still living at home and had not married yet, he also spent time in town.

On one of these occasions when Rabun was in town, he saw Hank on the street. Hank came up to him and started blaming the Peteet's for his downfall. He started cursing and calling Rabun names.

Rabun, being a mild tempered fellow just walked away from him, and tried to ignore him, but Hank would not let it go and kept following him down the street. The further Rabun walked the louder Hank got.

Rabun said, "Hank I don't want to hurt you, so just go on and leave me alone," but Hank got louder.

Rabun walked in the Washington Hardware store, Hank still following him and cursing. But this time Hank had pulled out his knife and was holding it in his hand.

Rabun knew he had to do something, so he asked Jim, who was working behind the counter if he had a pistol back there. Jim said "yes" and Rabun said "let me borrow it for a minute," Jim handed him the gun. Rabun turned around and fired one shot at Hank, hitting him in the leg and Hank fell to the floor. Rabun handed the gun back to Jim and walked out of the store.

Rabun knew there would be some trouble from Hank over this, but he went on home.

When he arrived at home, word had already gotten there that a warrant had been issued for his arrest.

He knew he could not stay around for that, so he went upstairs getting a few things together and was about to take off when he heard the Sheriff downstairs talking to his mother. The Sheriff was his mother's uncle and probably was hoping he would not find Rabun. They were talking loud enough for anyone a distance away could hear him. This gave Rabun a reason for not going downstairs, so he slipped out on the balcony and jumped down to the ground. He was very quickly riding away, while the Sheriff was still looking around the house.

The Sheriff was not too anxious to catch Rabun because everyone knew that Hank was always causing trouble and especially when he was drinking, and lately it seemed like it was most of the time.

Several weeks had passed and Ms. Martha finally received a letter from Rabun. He was in Ohio.

He had just gotten a job playing his violin in a band, he needed money to hold him over until he could get on his feet. Of course Ms. Martha sent it to him.

She also told him she would let him know from time to time how Hank was doing with his leg. Dr. Wise said the bullet did not hit a bone so he would soon be well. Mammy says he doesn't even limp unless he see's someone.

Rabun spent a year in Ohio, he was still playing in the band. He was going to parties and meeting a lot of pretty girls, so he was enjoying things as they were.

But something soon happened and his life was changed, he fell in love with a girl named Julie. It was his first love and he really fell for her.

One night he and Julie were going to a masquerade party, they were dressed in their costumes and were going to have a great time. He stepped out for a minute and when he returned he saw Julie and a fellow who had the same costume on as he did, leaving and going out to the garden. When he came close to where they were, he saw them making love. This was such a shock to him that he left the party and did not say anything to anyone.

Julie immediately realized that it was not Rabun that she was with and quickly went to find him. She learned that he had left the party.

The next day she contacted Rabun to tell him what had happened but he was so hurt he would not even talk to her.

He left for home immediately and never saw or heard from her again. He had received a letter that day from his mother stating the charges against him had been dropped. Ms. Martha was happy to have him home again.

One morning Tu Saint went to the barn to do the milking and he found someone had already been there and milked one of the cows, he told Ms. Martha about this. This had happened several times so he thought they should try and stop it.

Tu Saint told Ms. Martha that he would put his spirited horse in the stall instead of the cow. This horse would kick even if you just raised a finger.

The next morning he went to the barn and he found a man's hat in the stall and a milk bucket that was crushed. He said the hat looked like one that Hank wore.

Hank dropped the charges against Rabun because he was not sure what they knew about him taking the milk.

CHAPTER 25

The Boggs boys had quit making whiskey except just enough for Ole Tom. He threatened to sell the place if they let him run out, of course they were not worried as they had heard that many times before, they knew their pa was just talking.

When money got plentiful in the south again, they were sure to start the still up again.

Ole Tom says they make the best because they got the recipe from him. It had been handed down for generations.

Stovepipe was telling around that he knew those Yankee soldiers was lying all the time. He knew there was no place like Beulah land and he just went along for the company. Says he can tell when someone is lying by looking in their eyes and most Yankees are lairs.

Pockets was not going to be out done, he says he knew that there was no place like Beulah land but he went along because Stovepipe did.

Stovepipe was getting a little tired of Pockets, jest listen to you, if you ain't something. You better git some smarts soon or I'm going to git Mammy to let me work some place else and maybe git rid of Ola May. She always says do this, do that or I'll tell Mammy. Pockets you is so dumb.

Tu Saint's job was about the same, except there were no more slaves, just negros share cropping. They were free to come and go as they pleased.

Tu Saint was just to be there if they needed

something and help them wherever he could. But if any of them got lazy and wouldn't work, they had to leave. This was in writing and each share cropper signed with their X and it was witnessed. This share cropping was going on all over the South. This was the only way they all could have survived.

Tu Saint and Mammy were to be married the following Sunday after he finished the preaching. They stepped over the broom.

This is a form of ceremony that was used when the slaves got married and they didn't want to change now. But when they went to town they were legally married. This could be called a double ceremony.

Mammy and Tu Saint were both almost seventy, but were as happy as two eighteen year olds.

Ms. Briarfield was able to locate her daughters boyfriend. The army told her the soldier that they had helped during the war was from Ohio. He had never contacted them so he didn't know that he was a father. When he found this out, he immediately came from Ohio and married Mandy. His brother came with him, fell in love with Matilda and they all returned to Ohio.

Ms. Martha moved Mrs. Briarfield into the big house and Mammy and Tu Saint moved in the Briarfield house, to give them more privacy.

Rabun had been home for some time now and he had met a girl in Washington. Fell in love and they married before long. Her name was Margaret Escoe.

They did not want a big wedding, for things were not so good now as they had been and everyone was just doing what was necessary to get by. The war had left everyone stripped and there was little left to work with. There were no slaves left, they were all free and working on the land Ms. Martha had let them use.

So Rabun decided he would start a farm of his own, only he had a lot of cattle also.

Rabun built his family a house on Black Creek. Ms. Martha wanted him to stay in the big house, she knew it would be his in time anyway, but they wanted a place of their own.

Raburn had a good farm and was growing everything. Unlike cotton, his money crop was cattle. He kept busy growing feed and vegetables. His mother helped him with money when he got low and he was always able to pay her back.

Ms. Martha's wealth was far from what it was before the war, she didn't seem to worry about it though.

There was an old saying, "The lower you go down in the valley, the better the view looks when you were on top of the mountain."

This seemed not to apply to her though, she was grateful for all she had.

CHAPTER 26

The Golden Years were gone now. Ms. Martha was hardly making enough to pay her taxes and keep things going on the plantation.

Pockets and Stovepipe had the same job except they were free, they couldn't tell any difference than when they were slaves. Ola May was still the boss and they thought she was meaner than ever.

Now Ole Tom Boggs had started getting sweet on Mrs. Briarfield since her daughters had left.

He would sorta clean himself up and on his way over to visit Mrs. Briarfield, he would pick a few flowers. This was a let down for Mrs. Briarfield because she considered herself highly above him. But she got to thinking that she might be able to get him to give her his farm. So she told him after a few visits that she would marry him. She said she would give him loads of loving if he would give her the farm.

Now Ole Tom, drunk or sober was no one's fool and besides he didn't know if he could stand loads of loving or not. Anyway he gave her a life estate in the farm and she lived there the rest of her life. She had no other place to call her own.

They had a wedding at the big house. Tom had never worn a suit and Mrs. Briarfield refused to marry him unless he wore something other than overalls.

It was a big event, lots to eat and of course lots to drink. Tom couldn't remember that he had been married, let alone who he married. Mrs. Briarfield didn't really care if he remembered or not, because he was married anyway.

She moved to the Boggs house, and started taking charge of the cooking and cleaning for all of them.

Rabun was working his farm and was making money from his cattle. By this time he and Margaret had three children. Charlie, the youngest and the only boy. Mae was the middle and Stella was the oldest. Stella was my mother.

The South was down and would never again be like it was before the war.

Rabun was still showing a profit from his cattle and things were going good. But then the depression of 1893 hit everyone hard. Cotton was five cents a pound and nothing was selling.

It was December and Christmas was getting close. Rabun told his children that things were not good and they would probably not be able to have any Christmas this year. There was no money. He had plenty of cattle for sale but no one was able to buy them.

It was Christmas eve, Rabun was walking around in the yard. A big pile of dirt was on the ground where he was having a well dug, he was just looking around in the fresh dug dirt. Something caught his eye, he could not make out what it was, it was shiny and at first he thought it was a brass military coat button. He reached down and picked it up and much to his surprise it was a gold nugget. It had been dug up when the well was dug.

He didn't say anything about finding this to the children, he wanted to surprise them. He took the nugget to Washington and sold it, it brought enough money for his family to have the biggest Christmas they ever had, he was also able to buy Christmas for the other children that lived on the plantation.

CHAPTER 27

It was almost springtime and things were beginning to get some better. Margaret and the children, Stella, Mae, and Charlie were out making a garden.

Margaret saw a little girl walking quite a distance away across the field. Margaret said "Stelle look, there's a little girl walking at the edge of the woods and she looks like you, her hair is the same color as yours and her dress is like yours." Stella's hair was jet black and very long. Margaret said it could be you.

Her Mother said "Stella call to her" and Stella said "Hello, what is your name?" The little girl did not answer, she just kept walking. Call to her again, her mother prompted. Stella said "Hello, where are you going?" But there was still no answer. The little girl turned and walked into the woods.

This upset Margaret as no one lived in or around the wooded area, she thought it must be some kind of bad omen. This superstition was a feeling that the whites and negros felt because they lived so closely together. Margaret said they should forget the incident and not talk about it again.

Fall had come, Rabun was in the field getting the hay ready to be brought into the barn.

He was putting hay on the wagon and Charlie, his son, was sitting on the wagon waiting for a ride to the house.

A black cloud was over head and a storm came up. Rabun climbed on the wagon and they quickly started for the house, when suddenly a bolt of lighting struck and hit the wagon, killing Rabun instantly and knocking Charlie to the ground.

Charlie was wandering around in a daze and by the

time help got to the field where they were, no one could find Charlie. He had wondered around for a couple of days before anyone found him. Charlie was taken to the house and put to bed. It was almost a year before he was able to speak again.

Margaret remembered the omen of the little girl in the woods.

Margaret was very grief stricken over Rabuns death, she knew she could not take care of the farm alone. Her parent's owned a little store and the post office in a small community.

Margaret knew she had to sell the farm. When everything was sold and it was all taken care of, she and the children moved to her parents home.

It was not long before things were not going too good and this situation was not only difficult for the Escoe's but also for the children.

Mr. Escoe was very strict and did not allow much from the children. As Stella was the oldest, more was required of her than was of the younger ones. She tried very hard so everyone would get along, but she was missing her daddy very much.

When she was allowed to go to the store, there she saw big barrel's of raisins and she was allowed too fill her apron pockets with them before she left, this she liked and she always shared them with Mae and Charlie.

But as Stella grew older her feelings did not seem to change. She felt she was not always wanted or loved.

There was an aunt of her daddy's that lived in a nearby town, Toccoa. She wanted Stella to come and live with her so she could be able to finish school.

The Aunt had never been married and had no children, so she could easily provide for Stella.

Margaret knew that she was unable to do much for

the children, so she consented for Stella to go live with the aunt. Stella was happy about this and she moved to be with the aunt.

The aunt owned a millinery shop, so Stella was able to have the things she needed and was able to associate with another class of people.

Stella was able to get a good education and later she became a school teacher.

She was a very pretty girl, and in her teens she was chosen to be the poster girl for Maxwell House Coffee. Her picture was seen on billboards through out the state and on ads for their coffee.

Later years she married a lawyer, he was also superintendent of schools and later became Judge. They were parents of six children.

Stella's family was able to visit the Peteet plantation in 1934. The big house was still standing and there were also rows of the slave cabins. You could almost hear the singing of the darkies in the fields, that my Mother loved so well.

Stella and her family lived in North Georgia. She loved the mountains and never wanted to live anywhere else. Stella died in 1973 and was laid to rest in the cemetery that was given to the community by the family.

Ms. Martha, Stella's grandmother, died in 1917 and was buried in the Peteet Cemetary that was given to the community. It is in Washington, Georgia in Wilkes County. She lived to be ninety-one years of age.

Years have passed now, and all that is left of the Golden Years are the memories.

The King Cotton that made them rich also made them poor.

There's a small clear voice in the distant asking, "Was it worth it all?"

No one today believes in slavery. After the war, there were thirty thousand men in their prime of life, that had left their land to fight, but never returned.

More men were engaged and more men died in the civil war than in any other struggle up until that time.

A Personal Note
by
Sammie Kaiser, Daughter of the Author

This true story was told to my father by his mother, Stella Peteet. Just before he passed away, he wrote this book beacuse he wanted all his relatives to know about his mother's life.

Stella Peteet was born on a Georgia cotton plantation that her family owned. The family was very wealthy, and the plantation included hundreds of slaves.

One slave took care of Stella from the day she was born. Stella called that slave "Mammy," and she loved her as her mother. Stella grew up to become a beautiful and intelligent woman. She went to school, became a teacher, and later became a fashion model for *Vogue Magazine*.

She married a wealthy man named Russell Cannon Ramey and had six children. When she became a grandmother, she wanted her grandchildren to call her Mammy.

She died in Clayton, Georgia.

ABOOKS

ALIVE Book Publishing and ALIVE Publishing Group
are imprints of Advanced Publishing LLC,
3200 A Danville Blvd., Suite 204, Alamo, California 94507

Telephone: 925.837.7303
alivebookpublishing.com

www.ingramcontent.com/pod-product-compliance
Lightning Source LLC
LaVergne TN
LVHW060618110826
845147LV00019B/1046
9781631322730